AGILE SCRUM

CRASH COURSE

A Guide to Agile Project Management and Scrum

Master Certification PSM 1

UMER W.

TABLE OF CONTENTS

SECTION 3: SCRUM TEAM

SECTION 4: SCRUM ARTIFACTS

INTRODUCTION

Thank you for taking the time to read this. After all, time has become such a valuable gift these days. This book is for anyone who wants to learn the essentials of agile and scrum. It is also a great fit for those who want to quickly prepare for the Professional Scrum Master (PSM) exam. You can look forward to the following benefits by reading this book:

- You will learn all the important concepts of agile and scrum
- You will be able to apply agile and scrum on your projects and ensure their success.
- You will be very well prepared to pass the Professional Scrum Master (PSM 1) exam on your first attempt.

Agile has become one of the most widely adopted approaches to project management. Consequently, scrum is the most well-known agile methodology preferred by organizations around the world for managing their projects. In fact, these two terms are considered so similar that at times they are used interchangeably.

As a subject, agile and scrum can be challenging to understand. One of the major reasons is that most books that cover these topics are too complicated and do not immediately teach you the bottom line you're looking for. Furthermore, the language used in these books might seem too complex for beginners.

To address these issues, i aimed to create a book that welcomed people across the world from all backgrounds to agile project management. In this book, i have extracted the most important concepts and condensed them into an easy-to-read guide which you hold in your hands.

The book uses simple language to explain all the concepts in a clear and concise manner. This will help you quickly absorb the topics and apply the learnings in your everyday work. No matter what your industry background is, you will find it easy to relate to the examples.

This is the newest edition of this book and contains all the updates added to the latest edition of the scrum guide 2020. Some of the newer topics include the product goal, commitments, and an expanded section on sprint planning. To create a wholesome picture, this book contains information from multiple versions of the scrum guide and agile resources to create a complete understanding of what agile and scrum stand for.

Through this book, my hope is that you will be able to reach your professional, entrepreneurial, and personal goals faster.

I am absolutely thrilled to have you here. Let us begin.

BOOK OVERVIEW: WHAT
YOU WILL LEARN

Section 1: The Basics

In the first section, i will give you a complete overview of all the most important concepts of agile and scrum.

We will start by learning about waterfall and traditional project management.

Then, we will learn about what is agile. We will understand how it was started, why is it so useful, and what are the most important values of agile that can make your project successful.

After that, i will give you a complete overview of scrum. We will cover all the major rules and guidelines of scrum, including scrum events, scrum artifacts, and scrum roles.

Next, we will learn about sprints. A sprint is the most unique feature of scrum. I will give you a step-by-step walkthrough of each and every stage of how a sprint takes place on a project.

Therefore, the first section of the book is like a quick and comprehensive summary of the most essential concepts that you need to know about agile and scrum.

Section 2: Scrum Guide

In the second section, we will cover the Scrum Guide.

The Scrum Guide is the official document which was written by the original authors of scrum. It is considered as the definitive guidebook on scrum and is also the main resource for preparing for the Professional Scrum Master certification (PSM).

We will cover the topics in the same sequence as they have been discussed in the Scrum Guide to make sure you are able to follow the same flow and order of the content.

As you can see from the table of contents, the major scrum categories of scrum events, scrum roles and scrum artifacts have been divided into separate topics. By breaking down each section, we will be able to learn about other important scrum concepts in more detail such as product owner, product backlog, scrum master, and sprint planning to name a few.

The book conveniently divides and explains the subtopics in detail. To read up on any subtopic, just search for it in the table of contents and directly start reading about it.

My Approach:

You will often notice that I have broken down the content of this book into single lines instead of lengthy paragraphs. Please note that this is intentional, if you see a line standing on its own, it is considered as a vital piece of information for the concept being discussed.

The purpose is to break down the concepts into their sub-points to make it easier for you to take notes and easily recall them when you are preparing for your scrum master exam.

A BRIEF INTRODUCTION TO
AGILE AND SCRUM

Let's start with a brief introduction.

Agile is one of the most famous approaches to project management. It was originally created to ensure the success of software development projects. However, in recent years, industries from a variety of backgrounds have started using it for managing projects. According to a survey by the Project Management Institute (PMI), over 70% of companies are using agile for their projects.

Agile can be implemented in a number of ways and there are several agile methodologies, as shown in the diagram.

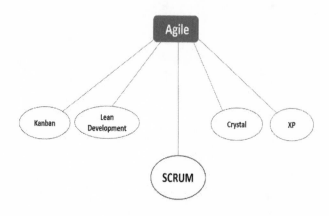

Out of all of these, scrum is the most famous agile methodology in the world.

So basically, scrum is the **most preferred way** of implementing agile on a project.

THE DEFINITIVE GUIDE TO PASSING
THE PSM 1 EXAM

What is Scrum.org?

Scrum.org was founded by the co-creator of scrum, Ken Schwaber. The organization provides trainings and certifications on scrum and agile. The PSM 1 is offered by Scrum.org and is one of its most famous certifications.

What is the PSM certification?

The PSM stands for the Professional Scrum Master, a highly recognized global certification. It can be pursued by anyone who wants to validate their knowledge of scrum and agile.

To be awarded with the certification, you must pass an exam by Scrum.org. Here are the details about the exam:

- Cost: $150
- Passing Score: 85%
- Total Questions: 80
- Duration: 60 minutes

- Question Types: True and false, multiple choice, and multiple answer questions

The exam is conducted online on the Scrum.org website so you may take it whenever you like.

You can register for the exam here:

https://www.scrum.org/professional-scrum-master-i-certification

Are there any prerequisites?

No, as mentioned earlier, you can write the exam any time you like, you do not require any additional training prerequisites.

How to pass the PSM 1:

1. **Read this book**

   I would recommend giving it a relaxed read the first time through. Just absorb and understand the information. On your second read through, highlight important information as you go over it. On the other hand, you could highlight the vital information on your first read through as well if you are short on time. See whatever works best for you.

2. **Read the Scrum Guide**

   Link: https://www.scrum.org/resources/scrum-guide

   This is the official guidebook for scrum, written by Ken Schwaber and Jeff Sutherland. The guide is relatively short. Once you've gone through my book, you need to read this.

Highlight key information that you read here so that you can revise it easily. Read it slowly and carefully.

3. Read the official glossary of Scrum

Link: https://www.scrum.org/resources/scrum-glossary

This is a list of useful terms; it is also great for a quick revision.

4. Revision

Revise the concepts until you can recall them easily from the top of your mind. You may use my book, the official scrum guide, and the scrum glossary for this purpose. Remember, it is very common to go through multiple read throughs, don't let anyone tell you otherwise.

5. Practice questions from Scrum Open Assessment

Link: https://www.scrum.org/open-assessments/scrum-open

The scrum open assessments are free practice questions from Scrum.org. The assessment contains 30 questions in the open assessment which are similar to the actual PSM 1 exam.

Important Tip: Complete the scrum open assessment multiple times. You will notice that the pool of questions will change and rotate each time you attempt it. Keep doing it until you start becoming familiar with all the questions.

6. More high-quality practice questions

Link: http://mlapshin.com/index.php/scrum-quizzes/

Mikhail Lapshin has created a very high quality yet free practice quiz. I would recommend doing the questions in learning mode, which will allow you to do the quiz without a time limit. Many thanks to Mikhail for allowing me to share his link here. This one exam is considerably more high quality than a lot of the paid options you would find online.

What is most beneficial about it is that each question covers a different topic. By completing this exam, you will be able to review most of the potential topics from the actual PSM exam.

Important tip: Make sure to read the answer to every question, regardless of whether you get it right or wrong. This will help make your concepts clearer and increase your chances of passing the actual PSM exam on the first attempt.

That's it, this is pretty much the most direct route you can take for passing the PSM exam on your first attempt. If you've done all the above, you should be all set for the actual exam, so go for it!

SECTION 1: THE BASICS

OF AGILE AND SCRUM

WHAT IS WATERFALL

Before we begin, it is important to understand the reasons why agile was born in the first place.

Since the early 90's, The IT industry was looking for a better way of developing software.

Before agile came along, people followed the traditional approach to project management.

This was also known as the waterfall approach.

So how exactly does it work?

In waterfall, projects are managed in phases. It was given the name waterfall because you complete the project in a linear sequence by moving from one phase to the next.

Phases of Waterfall

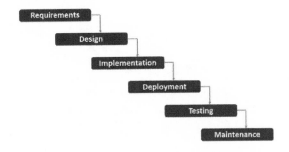

Let's take a look at the different phases or stages that a software project goes through in waterfall.

- **Requirements** – Gather the requirements of the software to be developed.
- **Design** – Plan the technical details e.g. the software architecture of the project.
- **Implementation** – Perform the coding and programming.
- **Testing** – Test the software for bugs.
- **Deployment** – Deliver the software and install it for the customer.
- **Maintenance** – Provide support and maintenance for the software.

Challenges of using Waterfall for Project Management

There were several problems with this approach which made it difficult for teams to execute projects successfully.

1. It only focuses on one type of work at a time

In waterfall, it is not possible to perform work from different phases at the same time.

You can only perform work on one phase at a time. For example, you will either do programming or testing, you cannot perform different types of work simultaneously.

2. Testing comes too late in the process

In waterfall, testing only begins once development has been completed. The issue here is that if we did not check for bugs while we were making the product, there is a chance we will carry over a higher number of problems later in the project.

3. Changes are difficult to make

Waterfall is not very flexible towards changes.

This is because at the beginning of a waterfall project, a detailed plan is created to identify all the requirements of the project.

All requirements must be known before we start making the product. You would mostly be expected to follow the same plan that you made at the beginning for the rest of the project. Because of this, waterfall does not welcome revisions or unexpected changes to happen at a later stage of the project.

Furthermore, it is very difficult to make changes in waterfall, especially when it comes to making corrections or fixes to previous phases. For example, if you were working on the implementation phase and realized there is a problem in the design phase, it would not be easy to go back and fix your mistake.

To correct your mistake, you would have to restart the design phase and complete its work all over again. This could result in increased costs and a delayed schedule for your project.

4. Delay in product delivery

Waterfall takes a long time to deliver the product to the customer.

You have to wait for all the phases of waterfall to get completed before you get to see a working product in your hands.

5. Lack of customer involvement

Clients only get to interact with the project team at the beginning of the project, when they are providing all the requirements, and then, at the end of the project, when they are receiving the completed product. The issue is that clients don't get the opportunity to provide feedback while the project work is actually being performed.

Result

Waterfall projects were unable to fulfill the most up to date business needs of the customers. As a result, the projects would end up getting cancelled or delayed.

The reality is that in today's world customer requirements and market dynamics change rapidly. Because of these reasons, it is important to be able to adjust project requirements and project goals quickly.

It would be unrealistic to manage software projects as a linear process; they are not an assembly line where you can do everything in a sequence without expecting the project to transform and evolve.

Therefore, traditional project management methods like waterfall are not fast enough to adapt to today's rapidly changing business needs.

All right good job. Now that you have learned about traditional project management, it will be easier to understand the benefits of agile and scrum.

WHAT IS AGILE

Agile was created because of the disadvantages of the waterfall method. In 2001, a group of 17 of some of the best software development leaders had a meeting in which they discussed better ways of developing software. As a result of their initial meeting, they agreed on a set of values and principles, which is now known as the Agile Manifesto.

This manifesto provides the basis / foundation for agile. They also created an organization by the name of Agile Alliance with the goal of promoting the use of agile across the industry.

So what exactly is agile used for?

Agile is an alternative approach to managing projects. It was specially created for managing projects in fast paced and constantly changing environments.

While agile became famous for its usage in IT and software development, its popularity is rapidly spreading to other industries, including automotive, construction, and finance to name a few.

You can think of agile as a flexible approach to project management. It allows project teams to quickly adapt to situations and make changes to ensure the success of the project.

Furthermore, it also allows you to develop working software early in the projects' life and deliver it into the hands of the customer so they can check if it is according to their requirements.

According to the Agile Alliance:

"Agile is the ability to create and respond to change. It is a way of dealing with, and ultimately succeeding in, an uncertain and turbulent environment."

Source: https://www.agilealliance.org/agile101/

Agile Values

There are 4 very important values of agile listed in the Agile Manifesto. Let's discuss each of them one by one:

The 4 Values of Agile

- **Individuals and Interactions**

- **Working Software**

- **Customer Collaboration**

- **Responding to Change**

Individuals and Interactions

First, agile emphasizes individuals and interactions, which means it recognizes the importance of good working relationships.

It encourages team members to have face to face and direct communication between one another instead of relying on strict processes and tools. This helps them solve problems faster and become more effective as a team.

Working Software

Secondly, agile focuses on developing working software as early as possible, which usually means at the end of every sprint. Excessive documentation can slow down project teams. Therefore, rather than writing out detailed documentation about the project, you are instead encouraged to focus on creating the product.

By quickly delivering an actual working piece of the product, the customer ends up being more satisfied. This is because the customer can check early on during the projects life, whether the product fulfils their requirements or not.

Customer Collaboration

Agile sets a high priority for customer collaboration. You are encouraged to work closely with the customer right from the start and then throughout the rest of the project. The project team regularly involves the customer while making the product and asks for feedback in every sprint.

Responding to Change

The last and most important value of agile, is responding to change.

Agile and scrum can respond to changes quickly. It is important to realize that projects are not that straightforward anymore. Changes can come from anywhere and at any time. Let's say that you're working on a project in which you're developing a new product. Consider that you're developing a new software, or a new sports car. Think about what changes can happen while you're working on your project:

- Your competitor might launch a new product with better features and a lower price.
- Your industry might shift to using a new product development technology, making the older one obsolete.
- Your customer might come to you in the middle of the project and say they want to change the direction of the project. They might also request that they want to add multiple new features.

All these changes in the environment make it necessary for you to react quickly and implement changes to your project. If you don't take any action in response to the external changes, your project runs the risk of becoming outdated.

It is important to keep up with the pace of today's fast-moving world. That is why agile and scrum not only expect, but also welcome changes to happen at any time on the project.

THE 12 PRINCIPLES OF AGILE

Agile consists of 12 guiding principles that form the basis for supporting project teams.

These principles help guide project teams to complete their projects with agility. We will go over all these principles along with a brief explanation for each of them.

1. Our highest priority is to satisfy the customer through early and continuous delivery of valuable software.
It is important to regularly provide customers with working software as soon as possible instead of making them wait a long time.

2. Welcome changing requirements, even late in development. Agile processes harness change for the customer's competitive advantage.
This means you should not be afraid of making changes even if your project is at an advanced/later stage in development. As long as the change benefits the customer, you should try to implement it.

3. Deliver working software frequently, from a couple of weeks to a couple of months, with a preference to the shorter timescale.
Agile works in sprints to quickly develop and deliver software that actually works instead of getting stuck in a lot of documentation.

4. Business people and developers must work together daily throughout the project.

This means that there are a lot of benefits to having business and technical teams working together because you end up with a better product that fulfils both business and technical requirements.

5. Build projects around motivated individuals. Give them the environment and support they need and trust them to get the job done.

In agile, teams are self-reliant, and they do the work by themselves. There is no need for micromanagement.

Instead, it is important to motivate and support the teams by giving them what they need to get the job done.

6. The most efficient and effective method of conveying information to and within a development team is face-to-face conversation.

Face to face communication is the most effective form of communication and is highly recommended for agile projects.

Also, it is important for agile teams to be collocated as it helps them develop a better understanding between themselves and increases their productivity as a team.

7. Working software is the primary measure of progress.

Delivering working software is the most important objective and is the main KPI (Key Performance Indicator). If your software/product doesn't work at the end of the day, then you haven't achieved your objective.

8. Agile processes promote sustainable development. The sponsors, developers, and users should be able to maintain a constant pace indefinitely.

Teams can be working on projects for quite a long time. They should maintain a reasonable speed at which they're able to deliver quality work without being burned out.

The lesson is that you shouldn't take on more work than what you're able to do and neither should you take on lesser work when you have a capacity for doing more, it needs to be just right.

9. Continuous attention to technical excellence and good design enhances agility.

Teams should constantly improve the quality of the product as it can eventually help them save time in the long run. There should be a focus on doing good work properly so that you don't have to spend a lot of time redoing the work or making corrections later.

10. Simplicity is essential--the art of maximizing the amount of work not done

Avoid doing work that doesn't matter. Don't dwell on extraneous tasks. Only work on things that matter that bring about the most value.

11. The best architectures, requirements, and designs emerge from self-organizing teams.

In agile, teams are empowered to set their own objectives while working and come up with their own unique solutions to problems.

12. At regular intervals, the team reflects on how to become more effective, then tunes and adjusts its behavior accordingly.

The teams should regularly inspect and check their work to see if it is going in the right direction.

They should focus on identifying improvements and make adjustments quickly to improve the performance of the project. In scrum, the teams usually perform these checks and balances at key meetings such as the daily scrum, sprint review, and sprint retrospective.

Source: https://www.agilealliance.org/agile101/12-principles-behind-the-agile-manifesto/

WHAT IS SCRUM

In this section, we're going to get a complete overview of scrum and its most important features.

First, let's start by discussing what exactly is scrum?

Scrum is a subset of agile, it is one of the most popular ways of implementing agile on a project. Over the years, the scrum guide has described scrum in various ways. Here are some of those descriptions:

- "Scrum is a lightweight framework that helps people, teams and organizations generate value through adaptive solutions for complex problems."

- "Scrum is a framework for developing, delivering, and sustaining complex products."

- "Scrum is a framework through which people can address complex adaptive problems, while productively and creatively delivering products of the highest value."

So in simple words, scrum is a set of guidelines and rules that allows us to manage complicated projects in rapidly changing environments.

Scrum has been used for product development, product releases, sustaining products, and identifying new markets and technologies just to name a few. It has especially been used in cases with heavy interaction between technology, environment, and markets. These days, scrum is being used in all kinds of industries and is venturing beyond its software development roots.

The Scrum Guide describes scrum as being:

- **Lightweight** - It is considered lightweight because it doesn't have a million rules to follow, it just has a few basic guidelines.
- **Simple to understand** – It is simple to understand because it focuses on how you can get work done and solve problems in the fastest and most straightforward way.
- **Difficult to master** – Lastly, it is difficult to master. In order for scrum to work, it is important to make sure its rules are being followed properly. If you don't follow the rules, you might not get results for your project.

The **benefits of scrum** can be divided into two major areas:

- It allows us to perform quick and efficient project management.
- It enables high quality product development.

Furthermore, being flexible and adaptive are the **key features of scrum**.

- **Flexible:** Scrum is flexible as it allows us to develop products while being open to change at all times.

- **Adaptive:** Scrum is adaptive as it helps us make changes as quickly as possible. It encourages us to change and evolve our approach towards managing the project in the best way possible.

Scrum Framework

Next, we're going to learn about the scrum framework. This is where we will explore the biggest components of scrum.

Scrum Team	Scrum Events	Scrum Artifacts
• Product Owner	• The Sprint	• Product Backlog
• Scrum Master	• Sprint Planning	• Sprint Backlog
• Development Team	• Daily Scrum	• Increment
	• Sprint Review	
	• Sprint Retrospective	

The scrum framework contains 3 main categories:

- **Scrum Team** – The specific roles and people involved in the scrum team
- **Scrum Events** – The events which take place in a scrum-based project
- **Scrum Artifacts** – The important documents and assets used in scrum

In the upcoming chapters, we will discuss each of these categories one by one.

SCRUM TEAM

The scrum team refers to the people who are responsible for completing and delivering the scrum project. Let's learn more about the members of the scrum team and their responsibilities. The roles on the scrum team include:

1. Product Owner

2. Scrum Master

3. Development Team/Developers

1. Product Owner (PO)

The product owner defines the features of the product and sets the direction for what needs to be done on the project. The responsibilities of the product owner include being a representative of the customer and managing the product backlog.

a) Representative of the customer

First, the product owner is a representative of the customer.

In simple words, he/she is responsible for understanding the customer's requirements and then clearly sharing those requirements with the development team.

b) Manages the Product Backlog

Secondly, the product owner creates and manages the product backlog. The product backlog is a list of all the work that needs to be done on the project.

Therefore, the product owner prioritizes what needs to be made on the project and acts as a bridge between the customer and the development team.

2. Scrum Master

The scrum master is the manager of the scrum process. This is the person who ensures everyone is following scrum rules on the project. The scrum master also provides help and support to the team by solving their problems.

3. Development Team/Developers

The development team/developers are the people who create and develop the features of the product. So basically, they are the ones who perform the actual work on the project e.g. programming, designing and testing.

What is the meaning of the word "Development" in Scrum?

In scrum, the word development refers to complex or challenging work. Development does not only refer to programming or coding. It includes any type of work that is challenging or difficult to do. This means that even though scrum was created for the software industry, it can be applied to industries beyond software.

Scrum Teams and their unique features

According to the Scrum Guide, the essence of scrum is a small team of people. This team is highly flexible and adaptive.

Overall, the scrum team typically comprises of 10 or lesser members. Projects can get complicated when there are too many team members. Scrum solves this problem by having a smaller team with highly qualified individuals who quickly adapt and respond to changes.

Scrum team members can be considered as **generalizing specialists.** Each member is an expert who knows a lot about one specific thing, and at the same time, also knows a little about a wide range of topics. Scrum helps make the most optimal decisions as it allows you to leverage the knowledge and experience of the entire team.

Scrum teams are independent and have a lot of authority to make decisions on their own. This enables them to quickly respond to changes in the market, product, and the environment.

Furthermore, scrum teams inspect and adapt the project based on feedback. What does it mean to inspect and adapt the project? In simple words, it means that every time you complete your work in scrum, you also inspect to check it and then ask the customer for feedback. The inspection and feedback allows you to adapt and make changes to the project. This loop of inspection and adaptation helps the team ensure that the products they're developing meet the requirements of the customer and the market.

SCRUM EVENTS

Scrum contains a series of events which are carried out across the duration of the project. The purpose of these events is to allow the team to plan, inspect and adapt, make adjustments, and track the progress of the project. Basically, the entire process of completing and managing the project takes place within the scrum events.

Scrum contains 4 formal events, which are contained within a bigger event, which in turn is called a sprint. Let's take a look at the different events which take place in scrum and the purpose of each event:

- Sprint

    - Sprint Planning

    - Daily Scrum

    - Sprint Review

    - Sprint Retrospective

Sprint

The sprint is a fixed period of time where a specific amount of work is completed. Sprints can also be considered as cycles of work where the product is developed over multiple iterations. The sprint is the bigger event within which all the other scrum events are contained.

Sprint Planning

A sprint starts with the sprint planning meeting. In this meeting, the scrum team chooses what they will work on during the sprint. In other words, this is where the scrum team selects the product features they will make for the current sprint.

Daily Scrum

As the name suggests, the daily scrum is a day to day meeting where the development team discusses the progress of the project. It gives the development team a chance to adjust and adapt their plan for the upcoming work.

Sprint Review

The sprint review meeting is an opportunity to check and evaluate the work done in the sprint. It is attended by the scrum team and different stakeholders (client, senior management). The scrum team gives a product demo to customer and receives feedback on the work they've completed so far.

Sprint Retrospective

Lastly, in the sprint retrospective meeting, the scrum team evaluates its own performance and suggests improvements to increase their effectiveness for future sprints.

SCRUM ARTIFACTS

Scrum artifacts refer to the documents and assets used on a scrum project. Each artifact is transparent and holds key information related to the project. Some of the most important scrum artifacts include:

- **Product Backlog** – This is the document which contains the overall list of requirements and features to make the product.
- **Sprint Backlog**– This is the document which contains items the team has selected for the sprint. It contains a small subset of the items selected from the product backlog.
- **Increment** – An increment is the outcome/deliverable of a sprint. It is the finished/completed piece of work you get at the end of a sprint.

Scrum Artifacts and their Commitments

The Scrum Guide mentions that each artifact contains a commitment against which progress can be measured. The commitments are the standards or yardstick against which you can measure the progress of the artifact.

Let's take a look at how the artifacts and their commitments are paired with each other.

1. Product Backlog – Product Goal

The product goal is the long-term objective of the scrum team and is the commitment for the product backlog.

2. Sprint Backlog - Sprint Goal

The sprint goal is the goal/objective of a sprint and the commitment for the sprint backlog.

3. Increment - Definition of Done

The definition of done is the quality requirement/standard for the product being developed and is the commitment for the increment.

WHAT IS A SPRINT - THE SECRET BEHIND AGILE AND SCRUM

Agile/scrum teams are small, flexible, and talented enough to take the project into a different direction at any time.

But the question is how are they able to adapt so quickly to changes?

The secret lies in the sprint.

Sprints are considered as the heart of agile and scrum, this is what makes them unique.

According to the Scrum Guide,

"A sprint is a time box of one month (or less) during which a done, useable, and potentially releasable product increment is created."

In simple words, sprints are used for building a product by breaking it down into small pieces. Sprints are completed within a time limit, one-month sprints are the most common, although this duration can be shorter as well e.g. 2 weeks or 1 week.

Each sprint has a goal – which tells you what you are making.

It also contains a plan – which guides you how to do the work to complete your goal.

Every sprint also has a list of items and features shortlisted by the development team on which they will work on during the sprint.

How a Sprint works:

In scrum and agile, you start a sprint by dividing divide a large project into many small projects.

These small projects are known as sprints. They may also be considered as an iteration, or cycle of work.

Sprint = Small project (Iteration / Cycle of work)

This is a very important point. Products will be developed over multiple sprints. You would make your way from one sprint to the other until you finally complete the entire project.

In each sprint, you will complete different features of the product.

Basically, you will create a certain chunk of the features of the product, you wont make the entire product in one single sprint, you will break down a bigger product down into smaller pieces, into its many features, and then you will create those features in batches per sprint.

For example, if your product has 100 features, assume that you're making 5 features per sprint. So if you're making 5 features per sprint, that means we will be able to complete the entire product in about 20 sprints. (Total features/Features completed per sprint. 100/5=20).

Once all the features have been completed, the work will be finished, and the product will be ready.

Example of a Sprint

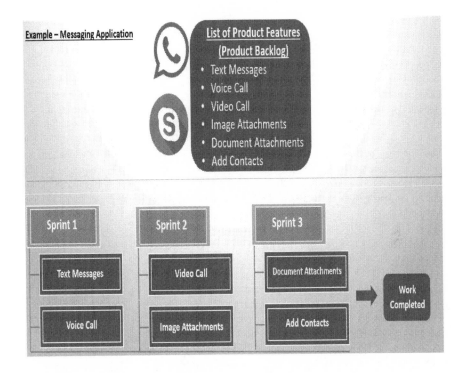

Next, let's look at an example for how a project is completed through sprints.

Consider that you're working on a software project, in which you're making an instant messaging application like WhatsApp or Skype. As you can see in the diagram, all the features of the product are presented in the list at the top, which is also known as the product backlog.

The bottom of the diagram shows you the different sprints which take place in this project.

Within each of those sprints, you can see the features being developed in each of them.

So, you would take the features from the list and develop them across each of the different sprints.

To create the application, we would have to make several different features which include:

List of Features

1. Text messages
2. Voice call
3. Video call
4. Image attachments
5. Document attachments
6. Add contacts

As we discussed earlier, you would divide the work into multiple sprints.

In this example, the work has been divided into 3 sprints, each of which are 1 month long.

There are a total of 6 items, so you are completing 2 features of the product per sprint.

In the first sprint, you would make the text messages and voice call features.

Then, in the second, you would complete the video call and the image attachment features.

After that, in the third, you will make the document attachment and add contacts features.

Once you're done with the third sprint, you will have completed all the features of the product and the product will be ready.

Advantages of Sprints

There are numerous advantages of using sprints on a project.

They are especially helpful for projects which have constantly changing requirements, like software projects.

Sprints provide you with several opportunities for making improvements. Towards the end of every sprint, the project team and the customer conduct a sprint review where they inspect the product and fine tune the project plan.

Every new sprint gives you the chance to make changes, include new product features and correct mistakes.

Because sprints are timeboxed to 1 month or lesser, you can show your product to customers earlier and more frequently compared to a traditional project management approach like waterfall.

Sprint review sessions provide customers an early opportunity to check if the product fulfils their requirements. If the product doesn't meet their needs or if the customer has new ideas and wants you to make a different product, you will still be able to quickly pivot and change the direction of the project starting with the next sprint.

Furthermore, sprints also allow project teams regular opportunities during sprint retrospectives to evaluate their work performance as a team and make improvements to the way they work for future sprints.

By enabling the project team to make improvements to the product as well as the performance and processes of the project team, sprints are invaluable for project management.

SPRINT WALKTHROUGH

As you may remember, the sprint is an essential component of agile and scrum. Let's take a step-by-step walkthrough of how a sprint takes place. This is a summary overview that explains what happens at every stage of a sprint.

The diagram below represents the entire scrum framework and shows the most important aspects of scrum. We will use a simplified version of the scrum framework to make it easy to understand how work is performed on a sprint.

Now let's discuss how a sprint takes place across a single cycle.

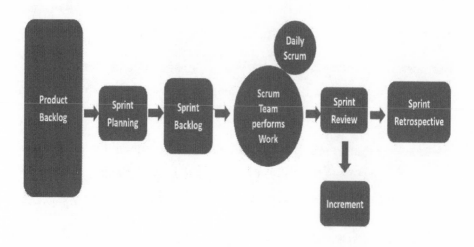

Let's cover each stage one by one.

Product Backlog

Before the sprint starts, the product owner has already created a prioritized product backlog. The product backlog is the document which contains the complete list of all the requirements and features to make the product.

When we say prioritized, we mean to say the product owner lists the most important features of the product at the top of the product backlog. So the items at the top of the product backlog are the features which the development team will be working on for the current sprint.

Sprint Planning

The sprint starts with the sprint planning meeting, which is the first official event of the sprint. In this meeting, you will make the final selection of what exactly are you going to work on in the current sprint. This means you will decide on what are the specific features of the product you want to develop in this sprint.

You would choose the features from the top of the product backlog; So if the product backlog document has 100 features, let's say you will pick 5 features from the top to work on in the current sprint.

Sprint Backlog

You will put these 5 features in a document called the sprint backlog. The sprint backlog is the document which contains the items which you have selected for your sprint. These are the items that the development team will work on and make them into fully functional product features.

Let's look at a quick example for how the sprint backlog is created. In the diagram, you can see that on the left, we have the product backlog, which contains the overall list of items and product features.

We will choose 2 items from the top of the product backlog and we will put these into the sprint backlog which you can see on your right.

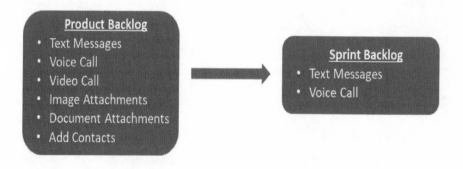

Scrum Team performs work – Development work/ Activities

Once the sprint backlog has been created, the next stage is referred to as development work or activities. This is where the development team will perform the actual work to make the product. In other words, they will be developing the features of the product. This includes activities such as programming, designing, and quality assurance.

Daily Scrum/Daily Standup

While you're doing the development work, you will also have the daily scrum meeting in parallel. This is a meeting in which the development team discusses their progress every day. Usually, the development team asks itself the following questions: 1. What are we going to work on today 2. What problems are we facing? 3. What we are going to work on tomorrow?

Increment

Once you've completed the work, you will get the outcome of the sprint. The outcome refers to the finished and completed product features you developed during the sprint; this is known as the increment.

Sprint Review

At this point, you're going to have the sprint review meeting. This is a meeting between the scrum team as well as the customer and other stakeholders like senior management. This is where you will show the work you've done so far and give a product demo to the customer and receive feedback to see if you're going in the right direction.

Sprint Retrospective

At the end of the sprint, you will have the sprint retrospective meeting. This is an internal meeting involving only the scrum team in which you will evaluate your performance and suggest improvements on the way you work for future sprints.

After the sprint retrospective, the current sprint will come to an end and the next sprint will start. It is important to note that there will be no breaks after the sprint retrospective, you will directly go into the next sprint. So basically, the entire process that we just discussed, will start all over again.

Summary: How does work get completed on a sprint?

Starting with the sprint planning meeting, the scrum team creates the sprint backlog by shortlisting items from the product backlog. The items in the sprint backlog are the product features which have been chosen for development in the current sprint.

The development team starts the work and completes the sprint backlog items during the sprint. As work is completed, the remaining work is estimated. Once you've completed a certain chunk of the work, you would evaluate how much time and effort would it take to complete the rest of the work. The development team keeps track of the project's progress by conducting daily standup meetings. The outcome of the work of the development team is an increment, which consists of fully completed and useable product features.

After that, the sprint review meeting takes place in which customers and stakeholders evaluate the product and determine whether it is being made according to their requirements. Lastly, the scrum team conducts a sprint retrospective at the end to evaluate their own performance and how they can improve in the next sprint.

You would then start the next sprint with a new sprint backlog that has been created exclusively for the new sprint.

You can check out the full scrum framework diagram from the scrum.org website here:

https://www.scrum.org/resources/scrum-framework-poster

SCRUM THEORY, PILLARS, AND VALUES

Scrum follows a certain number of principles and guidelines. These core principles can be divided into:

- Scrum Theory

- Scrum Pillars

- Scrum Values

Let's learn about each of these principles one by one.

1. Scrum Theory

Scrum is based on empiricism and lean thinking.

a. Empiricism

Empiricism stands for the empirical process control theory. The concept of empiricism says that knowledge comes from experience and from making decisions based on what is known and observed.

In simple words, it means that developing good products comes from having experience. For example, Sony uses their experience of manufacturing world class products. Because of their experience, they have the knowledge of how to create reliable products that can deliver a high standard of quality.

It also means that your project would be more successful if you were making decisions based on real time data and past information about the marketplace and the product you're making. For example, Apple and Samsung use historical information and use it to make new models of phones that appeal to users of the next generation. So using the most relevant facts, information and data helps you develop products which are a good fit for customers.

b. Lean Thinking

Lean thinking means that you should focus on the essentials, and only do what is most important.

Lean encourages you to reduce waste on the project by eliminating anything that is extra or irrelevant. It involves optimizing the value creation process by helping you create products with fewer defects in less cost, time and effort. By focusing on creating high value and essential parts of the project, you are more likely to be successful in creating a product that closely matches the needs of your customers.

Also, it is important to note that scrum uses an iterative/ incremental approach. This means that in scrum, you make something over repeating cycles. You work on, and constantly add features to the product until you've developed its final version.

2. Pillars of Scrum

There are 3 pillars of scrum:

a) Transparency
b) Inspection
c) Adaption

a. Transparency

The Scrum Guide states that:

"There should be a common standard so that observers share a common understanding of what is being seen."

This means that in scrum, everyone shares a common language. Everyone on the project should have a shared understanding of all that goes around on the project.

This applies to everything from the technical terms being used, to the products you're developing, to the different types of work each team member is doing. Each scrum member is expected to have an equal understanding of the project.

Furthermore, everyone should have a common definition of done. In simple words, "done" refers to the final and mutually accepted version of the product that the team is creating. Everyone should have the same idea about what the final accepted version of the product should look like.

For example, the entire team should have the same perspective about:

- What kind of software are we making?
- What are our quality standards?
- What kind of material are we using?

b. Inspection

According to the inspection pillar, you should frequently inspect scrum artifacts and progress. Inspection encourages you to perform regular checks to evaluate whether you have developed the product according to the customer's requirements or not.

This means you should frequently check and validate the product you're making, as well as scrum documents like the product backlog, sprint backlog, increment etc.

However, inspection should not get in the way of the work. This means that inspection is not something you should constantly obsess over every second. You just want to make sure you are doing the right work and creating the right product. You should perform checks and inspections frequently, but not obsessively.

Scrum recommends that skilled inspectors should perform inspections at the point of work. In scrum, there is no formal role for the tester, but it is better to have people who are skilled at testing to check the validity of the work at the place where the work is being done.

c. Adaptation

The adaptation pillar refers to quickly adjusting to and responding to a problem. On an agile/scrum project, it is very important to quickly identify deviations in the product and the project's processes. If there are any deviations, the team must make an adjustment as soon as possible.

For example, if you notice any products or processes are outside acceptable limits and do not fulfil your requirements, you should quickly make adjustments at the earliest to minimize future deviations.

If you ignore a products' faults in the earlier stages, then whatever you make in the future will be flawed as well. You should not continue to build a product that is flawed from its core. So basically, you should not carry problems into the future. For example, if you've developed a software and its programming is incorrect, then that incorrect code will give you more problems in the future. So it's important to quickly make adjustments so that you can set your project on the right track as early as possible.

3.Scrum Values

Scrum encourages its team members to embody the following values:

- **Commitment**: To commit to achieving the goal of the project and to be supportive of each other.

- **Focus**: To complete the work in the best way possible and to focus on the work required to complete the sprint.

- **Openness:** To be open and transparent about the work and the challenges being faced by the team.

- **Respect:** To respect each other and trust one another to be capable of completing the work successfully.

- **Courage:** To have the courage to do the right thing while working on challenging problems.

In the upcoming sections, we will cover Scrum Events, Scrum Team, and Scrum Artifacts. Each section will also cover additional concepts that will help provide more clarity for your understanding. The sequence of concepts we will discuss is primarily based on the scrum guide.

SECTION 2: SCRUM EVENTS

TIME BOXES

What is a Time Box?

A time box refers to setting a fixed duration of time to an event or activity. The most important thing to remember is that time boxes set a maximum duration which cannot be exceeded. They can be applied to any sort of event e.g. meetings or project work being performed.

An important feature of events using time boxes is that you would stop working when the time limit is reached and then you would evaluate what has been accomplished by that time.

For example, a sprint has a time box of one month. You would stop working on the sprint when the month is over, and then evaluate your progress at the end.

Benefit of using Time Boxes

The benefit of using time boxes is that it allows you to limit the amount of time spent on an activity. This helps ensure you don't exceed your time limit on the project schedule.

Work should be stopped at the end of the time box and progress should be reviewed. This could include:

- How many items have we completed fully?
- How many items have we completed partially?

When it comes to scrum, all activities are time boxed.

Time Box durations for Scrum Events

Let's find out what are the time box durations for the different events that take place during scrum:

Time Box Durations for Scrum Events

Sprint Planning Maximum 8 hours for a 1 month sprint
The Sprint 1 month
Daily Scrum 15 minutes every day
Sprint Review 4 hours for a 1 month sprint
Sprint Retrospective 3 hours for a 1 month sprint

SPRINT

A sprint is considered as the heart and centre of scrum.

This is where all the work is being done. In each sprint, the scrum team plans the work, performs work to develop the product, and conducts a review to evaluate the projects progress. Each sprint is like a small project where you create a piece of the product. It should be noted that this piece you create should be done, usable and ready to release.

- **Useable** – meaning it is a working product.

- **Done** – meaning it is complete and perfectly functional according to requirements.

- **Potentially releasable** – meaning the product is ready to ship to the market.

Sprint Events:

Each sprint contains a certain number of events. All the events listed below are a part of a sprint. They will take place in every sprint, no matter how many sprints you have.

- Sprint planning
- Daily scrum

- Development work / Activities/ Actual work performed to make the product in a sprint
- Sprint review
- Sprint retrospective

Note that while development work/activities is not officially mentioned in the scrum guide as a scrum event, however it is definitely a part of every sprint, which is why it is important to mention it.

Each Sprint will have:

1. A **goal** of what will be built

2. A **plan** for how to build it

Characteristics of a Sprint:

Let's learn the different characteristics of a sprint.

In sprints, you build on top of what has already been created.

This means that in every sprint, you're creating something new and adding it to your previous creation.

Let's say you're building a car. If you've made the body of the car, you will then add the tires to it. Basically, you're building the new product features on top of the previous features. You are constantly adding to the product in every sprint until you come up with the final and finished version of the product.

No changes will be made during the Sprint that can affect the Sprint Goal

Once the sprint goal for the current sprint has been decided, and if work on the sprint has been started, you cannot make any changes to it.

A customer might request for the addition of new items and features while a sprint is running. However, you cannot change the work in a sprint that is active. Therefore, those changes will not be implemented in the active sprint.

Any requests for changes will be noted down and added to the product backlog by the product owner. Any changes that are requested will be implemented in the next sprint.

Before the next sprint starts, the product owner will prioritize and organize those requested changes.

The product owner may bring them to the top of the list or to the bottom of the list, depending on the priority level of the requested changes/additions.

So remember that the sprint goal should not change during a sprint.

I would like to point out that small changes CAN be implemented during the sprint, only as long as they do NOT affect the sprint goal.

Generally, for the PSM exam, just remember that changes are not allowed during the sprint.

Quality Goals would not decrease during the Sprint

The team will not compromise on the quality of the product. The scrum team would never lower the quality for the sake of getting the work done faster, they would never use cheaper materials just so they can get over the project. Instead, they would always ensure they make products of the highest quality.

The scope of work becomes clearer during the Sprint

Once the team starts working and getting their hands dirty, they will be able to get a clearer idea about what they specifically need to do to make the product.

Having more clarity about the work will help the team make a better estimate about how much work they can realistically complete in one sprint.

The Development Team/Developers can renegotiate scope with the Product Owner

During a sprint, if the development team feels they will not be able to complete the work, they can renegotiate the scope with the product owner.

For example, if the developers had committed to delivering 10 items in one sprint, and after they start working, they realize this is a bit too much, they may renegotiate with the product owner to take on fewer items to develop e.g., 6 items.

Create a feature within one Sprint

Each product feature/user story should be created within one sprint.

It is not recommended to split it across multiple sprints.

For example, if you have an ecommerce website project and your customer asks you to create a checkout system.

You should make the checkout system within one sprint instead of completing it bit by bit across multiple sprints.

This is because splitting a user story can introduce risk to the project. Furthermore, during the sprint review, you can't show half done products, you can only show items and features that are 100 percent done.

Avoid short Sprints and very long Sprints

If you have shorter sprints on your project, chances are that you might not be able to complete your work. You would have to split the stories across multiple sprints and that is more likely to create problems for you.

On the other hand, if you have very long sprints, risks increase, and projects can become too complex.

Sprints help limit the risk of cost, time, and effort to a shorter time period. On average, it is recommended to have sprints that are 4 weeks in duration. 4 weeks are long enough to get work completed and short enough to help avoid risks.

When does the next sprint start?

The next sprint starts the moment the previous sprint finishes.

SPRINT PLANNING

Sprint planning is a meeting in which the team plans the work that is to be performed in a sprint. This plan is created by the entire scrum team.

There are 3 parts involved in scrum planning:

Why - Why is this sprint valuable?

- The product owner discusses how the value of the product can be increased in the current sprint. The entire scrum team creates a sprint goal that represents why the sprint is important.

What - What will be delivered in the upcoming sprint?

- The developers shortlist features from the product backlog to include in the current sprint.

How - How will we deliver the work in the upcoming sprint?

- The developers plan how to deliver the shortlisted product backlog items. For each item, the developers plan the work required to convert the item into an increment that satisfies the definition of done.
- Product backlog items are divided into smaller work items which should be completed in one day or less.

There are three important outcomes of the sprint planning meeting:

1. **Sprint goal:** The objective of the sprint
2. **Sprint backlog:** The specific list of tasks that need to be completed to achieve the sprint goal.
3. A plan for how the team will complete the work of the sprint.

Duration

The sprint planning meeting lasts for 8 hours for a 1-month sprint. For shorter sprints, the duration can be shorter.

Who attends the meeting?

The entire scrum team attends, including the product owner, scrum master, and development team.

The development team may invite other people from outside the scrum team to provide advice. This includes people from highly technical and specialized domains e.g. domain experts who can help the scrum team by sharing suggestions on the project.

What makes Sprint Planning valuable?

During the meeting, the product owner suggests how the product can increase its value during the current sprint. The scrum team works together to create a sprint goal that represents value as per the requirements of the stakeholders.

This helps the team understand the importance of the features they are developing in the upcoming sprint, why they are so valuable for the customer, and what significance they hold to the product as a whole.

Inputs to the Sprint Planning meeting

Before you can start off with your sprint planning meeting, you require the following inputs:

- Product backlog
- Latest product increment
- Projected capacity of the development team
- Past performance of the development team

How Sprint Planning takes place

We will divide sprint planning into different sections to make it easier for you to understand exactly how it plays out:

- Before the meeting starts
- At the start of the meeting
- Discuss the product goal
- Deciding the sprint goal
- Select items from the product backlog + make the sprint backlog
- Choose items according to team velocity/capacity
- Decide how to get the work done
- At the end of sprint planning

Before the meeting starts

Before the meeting starts, the product owner should ensure the product backlog has been groomed - this involves ensuring that the items have been ranked, ordered and prioritized with the most important work listed at the top.

At the start of the meeting

At the start of the meeting, the product owner shares his thoughts and:

- Discusses the objective of the sprint.
- Proposes which product backlog items can help achieve the objective of the sprint.
- Discusses which product backlog items can help achieve the product goal.

Deciding the Sprint Goal

After the product owner has shared his/her thoughts, the entire scrum team has a discussion on finalizing the sprint goal.

The sprint goal is the objective for the sprint. It provides guidance to the development team regarding the features/increment they will be developing for the product in this sprint.

The scrum team crafts the sprint goal together. The decision for the sprint goal is taken by all members of the scrum team together, not only by the product owner.

Select items from the Product Backlog to make the Sprint Backlog

By this point in time, the product owner has already ranked the items in the product backlog and arranged them in order of importance. The development team will now select the items from the prioritized product backlog. The development team picks out items from the product backlog and puts them into the sprint backlog.

The sprint backlog represents the items the team will work on during the sprint. These are the items that have been chosen for the sprint to create the increment.

The team selects items from the product backlog which can help in:

- Achieving the sprint goal.
- Developing the specific functionality/features of the product.

Let us summarize what we've discussed so far. We mentioned earlier that sprint planning is divided into the what and the how.

By this time, the team has completed the **What**. They have come up with the:

- Sprint goal – by defining the objective of the sprint
- Sprint backlog – by selecting the product backlog items for the sprint

Next, the team is going to focus on the **How.** During sprint planning, the development team creates a plan for how they're going to get work done.

The development team will start their discussion on making the plan for creating and delivering the items of the sprint backlog. In other words, the development team discusses how they will make the increment of this sprint.

Choose items according to team velocity/capacity

It is important to know how the development team decides the number of items it should take up for the sprint.

The development team is responsible for selecting user stories and tasks/items for the sprint. Note that no one can force them to take on more or less items because the number of items selected is entirely the development team's decision.

The development team makes this decision based on their velocity. They determine how many items can they realistically take on and complete in one sprint given their capacity, level of experience, skills and past performance.

I've discussed the concept of velocity in a separate chapter as well so we will cover it in more detail there. I touched upon it briefly here as it is a part of sprint planning.

How the Development Team creates the plan to deliver the Sprint Goal

After shortlisting the items for the sprint, it is now time for the development team to decide how to get the work done to complete those items. In other words, it is time to create the plan for delivering the sprint goal and creating the increment.

The plan includes information on how the development team will develop the increment, meaning how will they complete the product backlog items to develop a functionable product during the sprint.

To make the plan, the development team starts by breaking down the work into smaller units and creating estimates. They break down each of the large items into small and specific tasks. The team breaks down the tasks in a way that each of these smaller tasks should ideally be completed in a day or even lesser.

As a result, the development team will be able to determine how much time and effort is required to complete each item. Mostly, the work which is planned for the first few days of the sprint is broken down to units of one day or less. By breaking down the tasks, the team is also able to compare which are the bigger, smaller and medium sized tasks.

By this time, the team has created the entire sprint backlog, which contains 3 components:

= Sprint Goal + Product backlog items shortlisted for the sprint + Plan for how to deliver the sprint goal/increment

At the end of Sprint Planning

At the end of sprint planning, once the team has sorted out the planning, the development team explains to the product owner how it expects to work as a team to create the increment and achieve the sprint goal.

After this, the development team will start their work of making the items and creating the increment. So in simple words, sprint planning is all about:

- What are we making?

- Why is it important?

- How do we make it?

SPRINT GOAL

What is the Sprint Goal?

The sprint goal refers to the objective for the current sprint. It tells you what we are making and what should be achieved in the sprint.

Furthermore, the sprint goal provides guidance to the development team on why they are building the increment.

So basically, it helps keep their work focused. It makes it clear to the team that everything they're working on in this sprint, is related to that sprint goal.

Who makes the Sprint Goal?

All the scrum team members draft the sprint goal together.

Do note that the sprint goal will not change during the sprint. This is because it has been carefully finalized by the entire scrum team.

When is the Sprint Goal created?

The sprint goal is created during the sprint planning meeting, where it is added to become a part of the sprint backlog.

E-commerce Website Example

Let's say you're making a website where you can sell designer clothes.

For the current sprint, let's assume the sprint goal is to develop the payment and checkout system of the website.

To make this system, you need to develop different components.

First, you would need to develop the method of payment, where the customer would choose different types of credit card payment options e.g. Visa or Mastercard.

Then, you need to develop a section where customers can fill out their personal details, e.g., their name and phone number. Lastly, you need to develop the shipping address where customer would provide the location for where they want the product to be delivered.

- **Method of payment**
- **Personal details** → **Payment and Checkout System**
- **Shipping address**

As you can see, the payment and checkout system is a complete feature of the website which will only become functional once you've completed all these different tasks.

They key takeaway is that every task you're performing during the sprint, should be related to achieving the sprint goal.

DAILY SCRUM

What is the Daily Scrum?

The daily scrum is like a project status update meeting for the development team. It is held for a duration of 15 minutes. The meeting takes place every day across the entire duration of the sprint.

This is an internal meeting which is meant only for the development team. It is compulsory for them to attend and no one else participates in it. While it is not compulsory to do so, however the scrum master is free to attend the meeting.

The daily scrum is also referred to as a key inspect and adapt meeting. It allows the team to be in regular communication as they meet up every other day to share their progress. The meeting helps the team remove impediments and quickly solve problems. Because everyone gets to share valuable updates on a daily basis, they are able to identify and solve problems before they escalate.

In this meeting, the development team inspects the work done on the project and plans the work for the next 24 hours. It also helps the team to adapt/make adjustments to the sprint backlog and the upcoming work.

During the meeting, the team checks the work that has been done since the last daily scrum meeting. This helps analyze whether the work is being completed the correct way or not.

The team also uses the meeting to plan and forecast the work that is coming up. They discuss how they will perform the upcoming work in the next 24 hours.

The meeting gives the team a daily opportunity to evaluate progress towards the sprint goal. The team is able to track how many of the sprint backlog items have been completed and how many are remaining.

Furthermore, it helps the team become more knowledgeable about the project by becoming aware of how project work is going for every other person on the development team. This helps each of the development team members get a bigger picture of how the project is progressing.

Format of the Daily Scrum Meeting

When it comes to the format of the daily scrum, the team can either have a discussion-based session or the team members can ask each other questions. The most common questions asked during the daily scrum include:

- What did you do yesterday?
- What will you do today?
- Are there any problems preventing us from reaching the sprint goal?

The daily scrum meeting is held at the same time and place every day to reduce complexity.

Responsibilities of the Scrum Master in the Daily Scrum

When it comes to the daily scrum, the scrum master has some important responsibilities. Here are the most important ones:

- Ensure the development team conducts the daily scrum meeting regularly. However, do note that the ultimate responsibility for having the meeting lies with the development team itself.
- Ensure the duration of the daily scrum is kept to 15 minutes and does not exceed that time frame.
- Ensure other stakeholders do not disturb the meeting.

SPRINT REVIEW

What is the Sprint Review?

The sprint review is a meeting in which the scrum team shows the work they've done in the sprint to the key stakeholders. After showing their work, the team receives feedback from key stakeholders e.g. customer or senior management.

During the meeting, the scrum team inspects the increment and adapts the product backlog. The meeting allows the scrum team and stakeholders to evaluate the outcome of a sprint, and then decide what should be done next.

When does it take place?

This meeting takes place right after the team has finished working on the sprint.

Duration:

It's a 4-hour meeting for a 1-month sprint. For smaller sprints that last e.g., a week or 2 weeks, the meeting can be shorter.

Who attends the meeting?

The sprint review meeting is attended by the product owner, development team, scrum master, and stakeholders invited by the product owner. These stakeholders may include customers, business partners and members of senior management.

What happens during the sprint review and how does it take place?

The sprint review is an active working session where everyone collaborates on where the project should go next. The scrum team and stakeholders meet up to collaborate about what was done in the sprint. They work together to inspect the product and figure out how they can improve it further (in other words how can they optimize its value).

At the beginning, the product owner reminds everyone about the sprint goal – the objective the scrum team promised to deliver in the current sprint.

After that, the product owner discusses the status of the product backlog and gives everyone an overview of the progress made so far. The product owner also explains what items have been completed, and what items have not been completed yet.

Next, the development team takes over and shares their experience of the sprint: what went right, what problems did they face and how did they solve those problems.

Then comes one of the most important points of the sprint review. The development team gives a demo of the product by showing the current state of the product to the stakeholders. They also answer the stakeholder's questions about the increment. For example, the development team may be required to answer questions about the latest version of the product and all the new features they added in the current sprint.

The stakeholders check to see if the work has been done correctly. After reviewing the product, the stakeholders provide feedback. The scrum team can use this feedback to make improvements in future sprints. The stakeholders can also make change requests. They may request for changes or additions to the project.

At the end of the meeting, the scrum team and stakeholders decide together on what is the most important thing to do next. This helps in setting the direction for the planning of future sprints and what work needs to be done in them.

In the product demo, only 100% done items are shown. Only the items that are 100 percent complete and 100 percent functional are discussed with the stakeholders. This also means the scrum team only presents fully completed and releasable items for the product demo.

Also, the product owner ensures there are no half done or half-finished products being shown. This is because there is no point in reviewing items which are not complete.

The important thing to note about the sprint review, is that the team is presenting the work they've done while everyone inspects it.

During the meeting, the scrum team will collect input, feedback and change requests and will use it to modify the product backlog items for the next sprint.

In simple words, this means you will gather all the feedback and responses and note down the changes you need to make for the next sprint.

The product owner discusses the latest updates and changes made to the product backlog as a result of this discussion and will accordingly forecast probable delivery and completion dates of the product.

Basically, the product owner evaluates how much work the team is able to complete in one sprint. Then, based on that information, he/she can estimate how many more sprints the team would require to complete the product and the work e.g., do they require 3 more sprints or 5 more sprints.

Outcome of the Sprint Review

The end result of the sprint review is the revised product backlog. The sprint review provides input into what will be the probable product backlog items for the next sprint. So basically, it helps us define what work will we be doing and what features will we be developing in the next sprint.

In case there are any new features to add or changes/updates to be done on the product, they will be added to the product backlog and prioritized.

Responsibilities of the Scrum Master during the Sprint Review

Lastly, the scrum master has the following responsibilities when it comes to the sprint review.

The scrum master is responsible for ensuring:

1. The sprint review meeting takes place
2. The meeting occurs within the time limit
3. Everyone understands the purpose of the meeting

SPRINT RETROSPECTIVE

What is the Sprint Retrospective?

The sprint retrospective is a meeting in which the scrum team evaluates itself and finds ways to improve. During the meeting, the scrum team discusses how they can make improvements to the way they work for the next sprint.

The two most important goals of the sprint retrospective include:

- A self-inspection of the scrum team.
- A plan for improvements to be implemented in the next sprint.

Purpose of the Sprint Retrospective

During the meeting, the whole team will sit down and discuss:

- What worked and what went well?
- What did not work and what were the problems?
- How can team performance be improved in the next sprint?

Furthermore, the scrum team inspects the performance of the last sprint and evaluates the following key areas:

- People

- Relationships/communication
- Processes
- Tools

For each of these categories, the scrum team identifies what went well and what went right during the sprint.

Duration:

The sprint retrospective is a 3-hour meeting for a 1-month sprint.

When does it take place?

The sprint retrospective takes place within the time frame of the current sprint.

It takes place after the sprint review and before the sprint ends. So basically, it occurs before the next sprint planning meeting.

Who attends the meeting?

The entire scrum team attends the meeting, including the product owner, development team and scrum master.

Plans for Future Sprints

During the sprint retrospective, the team makes plans for making changes and improvements on future sprints.

To make these plans, the team focuses their discussion on two major areas:

1. Increase product quality by improving work processes

To improve work processes, the team asks itself the following questions:

- How can we improve communication and teamwork between people?
- What changes can we make to our processes to get work done faster?
- What tools can we use to develop a higher quality product?

2. Find ways to adapt the definition of done

The team reviews the definition of done and plans for how they can improve the DOD to make products of a higher standard.

Outcome of the Sprint Retrospective

The outcome of the sprint retrospective consists of the improvements identified by the team. The team develops a plan for implementing these improvements and puts them into action in the next sprint.

Why is the Sprint Retrospective referred to as a Lessons Learned Activity?

First, it is important for us to understand the meaning of lessons learned.

Lessons learned refer to all the things you learned from the project. This includes the key takeaways, the good ones, as well as the bad ones.

The sprint retrospective provides a formal opportunity for the team to inspect and adapt its work.

Basically, it is a proper and formal event that gives you a chance to evaluate your team's performance. This is the major reason why the sprint retrospective is considered a lessons learned activity.

The best part about doing the sprint retrospective is that you can take what you learned from the current sprint and then use that information to make the next sprint better.

In the next sprint, you can try to make improvements to your work and avoid making the mistakes you made in the previous sprint.

Difference between Sprint Retrospective and Sprint Review

The sprint review is a meeting that focuses more on evaluating the product and its features.

On the other hand, the sprint retrospective is a meeting that focuses on evaluating HOW the product was built. So the sprint retrospective is more concerned with people and processes and not on the product.

SPRINT CANCELLATION

Sprint cancellations are rare and uncommon. This is because sprints are already meant to have a short duration, so it is highly unlikely for a sprint to be cancelled.

Who has the authority to cancel a Sprint?

Only the product owner has the authority to cancel a sprint.

Reasons for Cancelling a sprint

Sprints can be cancelled when the sprint goal becomes obsolete. This can happen due to various reasons like technology changes or marketplace changes.

For example, lets assume you're developing a game for the Ipad. If you find out the next day that Apple releasing a new version of the Ipad which is not compatible with your game, you would have to cancel the sprint.

What happens when a sprint is cancelled?

When a sprint is cancelled, the completed and done items are reviewed.

Based on the review, only potentially releasable items are accepted.

Any incomplete items will not be accepted. They will be re-estimated and returned to the product backlog.

SECTION 3: SCRUM TEAM

SCRUM TEAM OVERVIEW AND CHARACTERISTICS

The scrum team is a small team of people who are responsible for completing the project. The team is empowered enough to manage their own work and manages all product related activities. This includes research, development, maintenance, operations, stakeholder engagement, and everything related to the product. The scrum team is accountable for creating a useable increment in every sprint.

Scrum Team Roles

There are 3 different roles that make up a scrum team.

- Product owner
- Scrum master
- Development team/Developers

Scrum Team Size: Typically 10 or fewer members

Are there any other roles in Scrum?

The scrum team only contains 3 roles: one scrum master, one product owner, and developers. Apart from these, there are no other roles in scrum.

Furthermore, a scrum team does not contain any hierarchies or sub teams. All the roles work in parallel to each other and no one is above or below one another.

Why do Scrum teams have such few roles?

Scrum teams are agile, this means they are meant to be faster and more productive.

A small team size enables the scrum team to have better communication, higher productivity, and the ability to quickly adapt to changes.

A smaller number of roles on the team makes it simple to identify who is responsible for what specific tasks and allows the team members to work and communicate with each other faster.

On the other hand, larger teams can slow down project progress and make communication complicated. Having more roles and members on a team can lead to challenges in coordination, miscommunication, and decreased productivity.

Teams in scrum are designed according to the scrum team model. According to this model, scrum teams are optimized to be flexible, creative, and productive.

Scrum teams Characteristics

Next, lets learn about what are the characteristics of a scrum team:

- Self-organized/Self Managing
- Cross-functional

1. Self-Organized / Self Managing

Scrum teams are self-organized and self-managing. This means they manage their work on their own and make their decisions internally. The teams choose the best way to do the work by themselves instead of being directed by others.

The development team decides within itself who is going to do what work. They are not managed by anyone and nobody orders them around. There is no manager who can tell each member of the team what they're supposed to do.

It is also important to note that the product owner or scrum master cannot dictate or give orders to the development team.

Note: The new scrum guide (2020) uses the word self-managing instead of self-organized. There is now a greater focus on the scrum team determining who, what, and how. Meaning, who will do what piece of work, and how will they do it. The overall meaning of the terms remains similar with the conclusion that scrum teams make their own decisions.

2. Cross Functional

Scrum teams are cross-functional, which means they are highly skilled and multi-talented.

Furthermore, scrum teams usually have all the competencies and skills needed to complete the work. They mostly don't depend on people outside the team and can handle the work by themselves.

The team members can take on multiple roles, they are not restricted to doing one specific thing.

E.g. Programmer + Tester

For example, a programmer can work on coding and also perform the role of testing the product by doing quality assurance.

What if there's too much work to handle?

If there's too much work to handle and if the team feels they do not have the capacity to handle such a large amount of work, then they have two options:

1. They can take items out of the product backlog, meaning they can remove some features of the product. In this case, the team should keep the most important features of the product and re-move the items with lesser priority.
2. They can hire more people, meaning they can add more team members on the development team who can help take on the work. However, please do remember that usually scrum teams are expected to handle all the work on their own since all the team members are highly skilled and capable.

Who are the stakeholders?

Stakeholders include the people who interact with the scrum team and may have influence or interest in the product being developed. They can provide support, guidance, requirements, and resources for the project.

Stakeholders may be internal or external and include roles such as the project sponsor, customers and end users.

Internal Stakeholders

Internal stakeholders involve employees, managers, directors, and the CEO of the organization. Stakeholders can be involved on a project in different ways. For example, the directors or the executive team could be the sponsor for the project. Developers working on other projects can share their expertise and suggestions with the scrum team.

External Stakeholders

External stakeholders include customers. The customer is a major stakeholder. Customers are not part of the scrum team, but they are of actively involved in an agile project. They provide the requirements for the product being developed. They also share feedback on the scrum team's progress and the work that has been completed.

Customers are often the end user; these are the people for whom you are making the product and who will use the product you are developing.

The CEO, directors, and the customers are just some of the examples of stakeholders. People from outside the scrum team are all stakeholders.

The product owner represents the interests of the customer. It is up to the product owner to make sure the requirements of the customers are made and fulfilled.

How can the customer request for changes on the Project?

If the customer wants any changes made on the project, they can share their request with the team and the product owner.

Then, it is the product owner's responsibility to update the product backlog and get those changes implemented by the development team.

Who is the Project Manager (PM) in Scrum?

There is NO official project manager in scrum. None of the roles in scrum match the exact role and responsibilities of a PM. The scrum master is not a project manager neither is the product owner a PM.

Since there is no project manager, the responsibilities of a traditional project manager are split amongst the 3 roles.

The development team performs the work and creates the deliverables. The product owner looks after project scope and manages the product backlog. The scrum master facilitates scrum events, provides support to the team by solving their problems, and ensures scrum is being properly followed on the project.

What happens when the scrum team meets for the first time?

When the scrum team comes together for the first time, they introduce themselves by sharing their background and profile. They talk about their skills and work experience.

This introductory activity is very helpful for the team as it allows them to decide the right fit of work for every member. It helps the team understand the strengths of every member and decide how the work should be allocated amongst the different team members.

After the introductions, the product owner shares information on:

- The Product
- Project goals
- Project requirements

The product owner also answers questions from the team to deliver as much clarity about the product as possible.

PRODUCT OWNER

Who is the Product Owner?

According to the Scrum Guide, there are two important responsibilities of the product owner:

- Being the sole person responsible for managing the product backlog
- Maximizing the value of the work of the development team

Let's explore the product owner's role in more detail.

Product Owner – Representative of the Customer

On an agile project, the product owner represents the customer. They are very knowledgeable about the customers business and requirements.

Furthermore, they act as a bridge between the business and technical side. They are responsible for understanding the requirements of the customers and sharing them with the development team in simple language that can be easily understood. You could say the product owner is the middleman between the development team and the customers.

Managing the Product Backlog

The product owner is responsible for developing the product backlog and is solely responsible for prioritizing the order of the backlog.

No one else can organize the product backlog.

Product Backlog Management Responsibilities:

Here are the key responsibilities of the product owner when it comes to product backlog management:

- Develop and clearly communicate the product goal to the scrum team.
- Create and clearly communicate product backlog items. The product owner should clearly share information on product backlog items. The product backlog items should be written with clarity and simplicity to make them easy to understand for the development team.
- Ordering, prioritizing, and ranking the product backlog items.
- Optimizing the value of the work of the development team by making sure they work on creating the most valuable features of the product before anything else.
- Making sure the product backlog is clear and transparent – this includes ensuring that everyone knows what the scrum team is working on right now, as well as what they will work on next.
- Making sure the team fully understands the product backlog items. The product owner should confirm that the scrum team, especially the developers, are clear in their understanding of the product backlog items.

The Product Owner and the Customer

Next, it is important to understand how the product owner works with the customer.

Customers are the people who will be using the final product. These customers/end users give the product owner a walkthrough of what kind of a product they are looking for and what kind of features in the product would help them achieve their goals.

The product owner lists down these user stories / product requirements in the product backlog. So basically, the product backlog is a list of user stories that are prioritized for value.

Prioritizing User Stories for value

The product owner is responsible for prioritizing user stories for value. This means that the product owner evaluates the most important requirements, and then places them at the top of the product backlog.

The development team picks these top ranked user stories/requirements and uses them to develop the product.

It is important for the product owner to make sure the user stories are easy to understand for the developers. As a product owner, you shouldn't use difficult language or buzz words. It is better to write down the requirements in simple words. This will make it easier for the development team to develop the features of the product and create a product that successfully solves the customers problems.

The product owner also measures the performance of the project. This means they evaluate the amount of work done per sprint. Based on the productivity and performance of the development team, the product owner is then able to forecast the completion date.

One Product Owner + One Product Backlog Per project

Next up is a very important point to remember.

There is only one product owner per project. You cannot have more than one product owner for a project. Also, there is only one product backlog per project.

While the product owner is just one person, however, the product owner can represent the interests of an entire committee of people.

Authority to make changes

Only the product owner has the authority to make any changes to the project.

Other stakeholders, like the customer or CEO can request for changes, but the final decision to make changes to the product backlog will be made only by the product owner. It is up to the product owner to decide whether to include any changes in the product backlog or not.

Furthermore, only the product owner has the authority to cancel a sprint.

Constant Communication

Now lets learn about why it is so important for the product owner to stay in constant communication with the development team and the customer.

While a sprint is active, the product owner should be available to the development team to answer any questions.

This is because the product owner is the one who knows everything about the customers' requirements. There are chances the project might go in the wrong direction if the product owner is not available to help the development team in case they want any clarifications or more information.

Also, the product owner must stay in contact with customers to keep the product backlog updated in case there are any requests for additional features or change requests for the project.

Respect and Authority

In order for the project to succeed, everyone should respect the product owners' decisions. For scrum to work properly, no one should override the decisions of the product owner.

The decisions of the product owner can be seen based on how they have organized the content of the product backlog. The arrangement and order in which the product backlog has been listed will give you an idea about what the product owner thinks is more important for the project.

The development team will only do the work that they have discussed with the product owner. No one can ask the team to work on anything other than requirements listed in the product backlog.

Delegating Work Related to the Product Backlog

The product owner can delegate work to the development team when it comes to the product backlog. For example, they can ask someone from the development team to write user stories. However, at the end of the day, the product owner is ultimately responsible and accountable for his/her own work.

Optimize Value

The product owner optimizes the value of the product and the work of the development team.

They do this by prioritizing the product backlog and focusing on features that are the most important to the customers.

The product owner ranks the most important features of the product at the top and the least important ones at the bottom. This helps focus the development team's effort on creating features on the product which:

- Offer the most value to the customer.

- Deliver the most benefits.

- Are the best solutions for the customers problems.

How to request the product owner to make changes on the project

If anyone wants changes made on the project e.g., the CEO or the customer, they must talk to the product owner.

The product owner will then include the request into the product backlog, prioritize it, and communicate that feature to the development team. After that, the development team will make the requested change or addition to the product.

To summarize, the product owner is:

- A product expert
- Facilitator of stakeholders
- Value maximizer

DEVELOPMENT TEAM

The development team is a highly skilled group of people who are responsible for developing the product. In other words, they are the ones who are directly involved in the actual work of creating the product. The development team uses the requirements listed in the product backlog to create the product step by step across multiple sprints. They create a useable increment in every sprint.

The development team usually contains experts who specialize in a particular area, for example, they can be technical people like programmers, coders and testers.

Development Team Size

The recommended development team size is 3-9 members.

Not less than 3 and not more than 9.

The reason for the 3-9 range is that it allows for easy communication and it allows the team to get work done faster. It is the optimal number that would allow the team to be small enough to be quick and agile. At the same time, it would be large enough to be productive.

If you have less than 3 members, there is a chance the team might experience less productivity due to skill constraints and they simply might not have enough expertise to create a working increment.

If there are more than 9 members on the development team, things will start getting complicated. More coordination will be required and complexity will increase. This goes against the spirit of an agile project because the developers would not be able to quickly react to changes and adapt to new conditions.

According to the latest version of the scrum guide (2020), the overall number of scrum team members, should be ideally 10 or lesser. From this, we can infer that the scrum master and product owner would each occupy one position on the team. That leaves us with a maximum of 8 positions for the development team/developers.

Development Team Titles

There are no titles in the development team. Everyone on the team is known as a development team member or a developer. There are no specific designations such as web developer, app developer etc.

Development Team Groups

There are no sub teams or sub-groups which have their own names. So, there is no programming team, Quality assurance team etc.

Multiple Development Teams

You can have more than one development team on the same project.

For example, for a large project, you can have multiple development teams working on different parts of the project.

It is also important to note that all the development teams should have the same sprint starting date.

Can the Scrum Master and Product Owner be part of the development team?

The product owner and scrum master can be a part of the development team. However, this is not recommended as it can lead to a conflict of interest.

Accountability in the Development Team

Here are the most important responsibilities of the development team:

- Creating the Sprint Backlog (the plan for the sprint)
- Ensure quality by following the definition of done
- Adapting the plan every day towards the sprint goal
- Holding each other accountable for work as professionals

You should always remember that the whole scrum team is responsible and accountable for the entire project. No single individual can be held responsible for one thing.

The development team consists of specialists and highly skilled people who are experts in their own areas. However, this does not mean they will be restricted to working on only one specific task.

Agile project teams are expected to multitask since most of them are generalizing specialists. A person who specializes in programming can also be expected to perform quality assurance and testing. So if something goes wrong on the project, no individual team member can say

"I'm not responsible for this problem" or "I wasn't even working on this task"

On a project, individual team members might be working on different tasks from one another. However, at the end of the day, what matters is the bottom line and whether the team was able to get the work done. So when it comes to responsibility, the entire scrum team is responsible and accountable for the success or failure of the project.

How does the Development Team work with the Product Owner on the Sprint?

The product owner and the development team get together to decide the tasks for the upcoming sprint.

The product owner shows the development team the most important product backlog items that the team needs to work on to achieve the sprint goal.

Then, the development team selects the items for the sprint.

The development team selects the number of items they want to take up based on their capacity.

After that, the selected items are broken down into smaller tasks.

During the sprint, the developers perform the work to complete the tasks.

Once all the items are completed, the development team gives a demo of their work in the sprint review.

An important fact to remember is that only the development team can decide how many items they want to take up for the sprint. No one can force them to take up the work.

How does the development team develop the product?

Let's take a walkthrough of how the development team creates the product.

First, it is important to point out that the development team works on a single project at a time. The scrum team members are not involved in multiple projects. This helps them focus and give their best to one project.

The team develops the product in chunks by creating increments through sprints.

Before the start of each sprint, the development team selects a chunk of items from the product backlog.

This shortlisted chunk of items that the team works on in a particular sprint is known as the sprint backlog.

During the sprint, the development team works on these items and develops them into a complete and functional product feature.

The outcome of the sprint is a "done" item, which in other words, is a fully functional and completed feature of the product. This "done" item is called an increment.

So the same chunk of work that is worked on during the sprint, becomes the increment once it is finished.

Once the increment is completed, it has to go through a review. If it passes the review, it becomes ready for release.

Reasons why there are no specific roles or sub team names in Scrum:

It is entirely up to the development team to decide how they want to divide the work amongst the team members. One person could be working on the same task across the entire project or they could be performing different task. For example, a person could working on only programming, or they could be working on programming, design, and quality assurance at the same time.

In scrum, developers are expected to be cross functional. They are not restricted to one specific function or role. This is why team members are not referred to as programmers, or designers. Instead, they are just referred to as development team members / developers.

The Team needs a common Definition of Done (DOD)

For the project to be successful, the entire scrum team needs to reach a common understanding of the DOD. This especially applies to the development team. Every developer should have a shared understanding of the criteria under which they would consider a task to be complete. The DOD needs to be the same across the board.

Everyone needs to have the same understanding as to what done means when it comes to the entire project, as well as each individual sprint. Having a common understanding will help ensure everyone is making the correct product as expected by everyone else on the team. It also helps decrease the margin for error and problems on the project.

Add on to what's been completed

In sprints, the development team adds on new work to what has already been completed.

Consider a situation where a team has just completed sprint no.1 and are now about to start work on to sprint no.2.

Every time you start a new sprint, you need to develop additional new features which are over and above what you developed in the previous sprint. This means that the team will not touch the work that has already been completed and released in the previous sprint.

Instead, the team will develop new features in the new sprint and add them to the features which were created in the previous sprint.

What happens in case the development team is unable to finish the items in the Sprint Backlog?

In case the development team is unable to finish the items in the sprint backlog in a particular sprint, the following things would happen:

- The incomplete items would not be included in the increment of the current sprint.
- The items would not be shown in the sprint review. This basically means that the items would not be shown to the customer during the demo which takes place in the sprint review.
- The items will be returned to the product backlog, and they must be analyzed again. The product owner will re-estimate and reprioritize what needs to be done with those items.

Development Team or Developers?

In the new scrum guide (2020), the term development team has been replaced with developers. This was done to remove confusion between the terms scrum team and development team. The word team was removed from development to eliminate the concept of a separate team. Its purpose was to emphasize that the developers are indeed a part of the scrum team and are not a separate team within a team.

However, the term development team is still used across several project management methodologies and is widely accepted and understood. This is why in this book, we will continue to primarily use the term development team. Note that both terms, development team and developers, are synonymous and refer to the exact same group of people i.e. people who do the work to create the product. Just remember that for the psm exam, you will see the term developers being used instead of development team. Other than that, there is absolutely no difference in the role or accountabilities between the two terms.

Summary:

The development team:

- Is Self-organizing/Self-managing
- Is Cross functional
- Recognizes no titles
- Does not have sub teams e.g. programming team, QA team

SCRUM MASTER

Who is the Scrum Master?

In simple words, the scrum master is the person who promotes and supports scrum by helping everyone understand its rules and guidelines.

This is the person who ensures the team and organization are following scrum in the correct way.

In order to understand this role, we need to look at how the scrum master interacts with the rest of the team. We will explore the following relationships:

- Scrum master and the organization
- Scrum master and the development team
- Scrum master and the product owner
- Scrum Master and the Scrum Team

Scrum Master and the Organization

The scrum master is like a representative of scrum in an organization.

They lead the organization to use and adopt scrum. They are responsible for ensuring scrum is being understood and implemented correctly.

Basically, they help people understand the scrum rules, values, theory and behavior.

Scrum masters share information on scrum through:

- Workshops
- Trainings
- Sharing online and offline knowledge resources like guides, books and tutorials

The scrum master is also a coach and a trainer, they ensure that the scrum team is correctly implementing the scrum processes. For example, when it comes to the daily scrum meeting, the scrum master ensures the team is carrying out the meeting every day. They also ensure the team is holds a time boxed 15-minute meeting and does not exceed the 15-minute limit.

Scrum Master and the Development Team

When it comes to the development team, the scrum master is a servant leader. This means that they remove problems that the scrum team is facing. For example, if the team is facing problems and hurdles in getting their work done in the organization, the scrum master helps them solve those issues. According to the latest scrum guide (2020), more emphasis has been placed on the scrum master being a leader. However, the concept of scrum master being a servant leader remains valid.

Source:https://www.scrum.org/resources/blog/scrum-guide-2020-update-what-has-been-removed).

Furthermore. the scrum master keeps stakeholders in check by ensuring they follow the rules when it comes to their interactions with the scrum team. The scrum master helps people outside the scrum team understand which interactions helpful and which interactions are not helpful.

In simple words, this means that the scrum master stops people from disturbing the scrum team and provides guidance on what is the right way and the right time to get in touch with the scrum team.

Stakeholders like customers and senior management can often try to get in touch with the scrum team in the middle of their work. Think about your own experience. You must have come across situations where the CEO, director or the customer immediately want changes to be made on the project, or they might barge in asking for an immediate progress report.

The key is, you can't allow them to directly just go up to the development team and ask them to do things right there and then. The scrum master should ensure the stakeholders don't interrupt the development team. It is the scrum master's responsibility to only allow interaction at the correct time and through the right procedure, e.g. during sprint review.

Therefore, the scrum master acts as a shield for the development team by helping them do their work without interruptions and interference.

Scrum Master and the Product Owner

The scrum master also plays an important role in helping the product owner. The scrum master helps the product owner:

- Define the product goal.

- Find techniques to effectively manage the product backlog.

- Organize the product backlog items to maximize its value.

Scrum Master and the Scrum Team

When it comes to the scrum team overall, the scrum master provides support by doing the following tasks:

- Guide the scrum team to ensure the backlog items are clear, concise, and easily understandable by everyone. The easier it is to understand the contents of the product backlog, the clearer it will be for everyone to understand what needs to be done on the project.

- Facilitate scrum events by setting up the different sessions of scrum including the daily scrum, sprint review, and sprint retrospective.

- Facilitate stakeholder collaboration. They facilitate the scrum team in getting help from the outside if the team ever needs extra support.

Is Scrum Master a Task Master?

A task master is someone who rigorously supervises the work of the team on the project.

The scrum master should not be a task master. As a scrum master, you should only focus on managing the scrum process, you are not there to manage the team and its daily tasks.

The role of the scrum master is a management position. However, scrum masters are not involved in managing people and are not responsible for delegating specific tasks to every person on the team. Instead, they manage the scrum process and ensure that scrum and its guidelines is being followed by the team members.

A scrum master should let the team organize itself and perform work the way it feels best. In case the team runs into any problems, it is the scrum master's responsibility to provide support and help them out.

What is the difference between a Scrum Master and a Project Manager?

Scrum masters are more like coaches to the team while a traditional project manager role involves managing the team.

The scrum master is not involved in leading the team, planning, delegating work or even making decision about the next steps of the project. All these are tasks which a traditional project manager would be involved in.

Can the Scrum Master be a Product owner or a member of the Development Team?

It is possible for a scrum master to simultaneously be a part of the development team or a product owner. However, it is not recommended, and it is better if their role is kept separate to help avoid conflicts of interest and misunderstandings.

SECTION 4: SCRUM ARTIFACTS

PRODUCT BACKLOG (PB)

The product backlog is a document that contains everything that needs to be done on the project. It is the most important document used in scrum.

The scrum guide states that the product backlog is:

"An ordered list of everything needed in the product and the single source of requirements for any changes to be made on the product".

In simple words, the product backlog contains all the information regarding the product and contains the complete list of requirements to make the product. Furthermore, the product goal, which is the long-term objective of the scrum team, is also part of the product backlog.

When you start making a product backlog for the first time, it contains the best understood requirements. In the future, it starts to include enhancements, fixes and changes that can be requested by the customer or stakeholders.

The list of items in the product backlog include:

- Product Goal
- Product features
- Requirements
- Functionalities

- Enhancements
- Fixes
- Changes

It is also important to note that the product backlog is the ONLY source of requirements for changes to the product. You can't implement changes to the product directly. Only changes which are listed in the product backlog will be implemented. This is why the product backlog is referred to as the only source which contains a list of all the changes which need to be implemented on the project.

For example, if the CEO or customer tells you to make changes, you can't just simply go right ahead and implement them directly. You can only implement changes if they have been added to the product backlog by the product owner.

Just remember that if an item is not in the product backlog, it is not a part of the project.

What is the Product Goal?

The product goal is the long-term objective of the scrum team. It may also be considered as the future state of the product. The product goal is the target based on which the scrum team will plan their work.

As per the scrum guide, the product backlog defines what is required to fulfill the product goal. To elaborate, this means that the product backlog defines the list of all the items that will contribute towards achieving the product goal. During the sprint planning meeting, the attendees discuss the most important product backlog items and how they are connected to achieving the product goal.

The Product Backlog is a Living Artifact

The product backlog is a dynamic document that constantly changes. This is because a project's requirements never stop changing. The product backlog is constantly improved because changes and product features are added regularly.

Whenever there are any changes required on the product, first they will be added to the product backlog and THEN the development team will implement those changes.

The product backlog evolves as the product evolves. That is why, as long as the product exists, it's product backlog also exists.

Based on the feedback received from the customers and the market-place, the product backlog grows larger as improvements and changes are constantly added to adapt to the current situation and demands.

It is important to note that the product backlog is never complete. The product owner will keep adding new ideas while older ideas might get removed. The document is regularly updated and rewritten to make sure it represents the current needs of the customer and the market-place.

What causes changes on the product backlog?

Changes can be added to the product backlog due to:
- Stakeholder requirements
- Market conditions
- Technology
- Business requirements

How many product backlogs are there for a product?

Only one product backlog is used for developing a product. There may be multiple development teams working on a product, but they will all use the same product backlog.

Prioritizing Product Backlog Items (PBI)

The product owner prioritizes the items in the product backlog and arranges them in order of importance.

The goal is to prioritize items in a way that optimizes the value of the work done by the development team.

In simple words, product backlog items are organized based on their priority.

The most important items are placed at the top. These are the items which the product owner wants the development team to work on immediately.

This is because the items at the top are the most important features of the product and provide the most business value.

Since the product backlog is a list, you should always remember that:

- Items at the top of the list are high value items. These items have a high level of clarity.
- Items at the bottom of the list are low value items. These items have a low level of clarity.

Let's look at an example to understand what this means. If you're developing a supercar, its engine would be at the top. The engine brings the most business value because it's the heart of the car, and it is the most valuable feature which allows the car to reach its top speed. Similarly, when it comes to software, the actual code of the software is one of its most important features.

Who makes the estimates?

Estimates are an important part of project planning. An estimate tells you the quantitative measure of costs and duration for making a specific item on the project.

The development team is responsible for making the estimates. Basically, the people who do the actual work of making the product will make the estimates. The process of estimation involves calculating:

- How much each item costs?
- How much time will it take to make each of the different items?

Why are items at the top of the product backlog described in more detail?

As discussed earlier, the items at the top are high priority items. They are described in substantial detail so that the development team can have enough clarity to start working on them.

Furthermore, it is important to analyze the items well in time and share enough details so that the development team can complete them in a single sprint.

Since high ranked items have more clarity and detail, they have more precise estimates.

Who is responsible for the product backlog?

The product owner is responsible for the product backlog.

There are 3 main responsibilities of the product owner when it comes to the product backlog:

- Content
- Availability
- Ordering

Content

The product owner decides what content is included in the product backlog. This includes:

1. Understanding what features the client wants in their product.

2. Including the features in the form of a list in the product backlog.

Availability

The product owner is responsible for making sure the product backlog is readily available to the development team at all times. Making the product backlog easily accessible and readily available is very important because this is the document the development team will use for making the product.

Ordering

The product owner is responsible for prioritizing the items in the product backlog. Prioritizing involves making sure that the most important features of the product are listed at the top while the least important are listed at the bottom.

PRODUCT BACKLOG REFINEMENT

Product backlog refinement is the process of adding order, details and estimates to the items of the product backlog. It involves breaking down and refining product backlog items into smaller and specific items. It is considered an ongoing activity as you are regularly adding more details to product backlog items.

The product owner and development team work together to:

- **Add more information and clarity to the items**
  This includes any information that can guide the team on the best way to develop the item. You can include information and details such as: What is this item? What are its requirements? What are its specifications?

- **Add estimates**
  This refers to adding estimates for time and cost. You can include information such as: How much time would it take to make this item? How much would it cost to make this item? The development team is responsible for sizing the items.

- **Set the items in order**
  This refers to deciding which are the most important items so that they can be placed at top of the list.

The process of product backlog refinement does not take up more than 10% of the capacity of the development team, so they don't spend a very large amount of time performing this task.

SPRINT BACKLOG

What is the Sprint Backlog?

The sprint backlog is a plan that is made by the development team. It contains details on how they will accomplish the work on the sprint. In simple words, the sprint backlog is like a picture of the work that needs to be completed by the development team to achieve the sprint goal. It contains:

1. **Sprint Goal (Why)** – The goal or objective for the sprint.
2. **Shortlisted product backlog items (What)** – These are the items which the team has chosen to work on during the sprint.
3. **A Plan for delivering the increment (How)** – A plan on how to do the work to make the items.

Now let's discuss it in more detail:

1. Sprint Goal – The objective of the sprint (we have already covered this concept in detail earlier.)

2. Shortlisted Items

While the product backlog contains information on everything to be done on the project, the sprint backlog contains information on ONLY the things that need to be done on the sprint.

Therefore, the sprint backlog contains the set of product backlog items which are selected for the sprint.

It usually contains items which are chosen from the top of the product backlog since the items at the top of the list are the most important ones that the team needs to work on. You could say they are the core features of the product you are setting out to make.

Let's take an example of how items are shortlisted from the product backlog. Assume that the product backlog has a total of 100 items. For the sprint, if the development team selects 5 items to work on, then these 5 items will be the sprint backlog.

Therefore, the sprint backlog is like a subset of the product backlog. It contains the set of items the team will develop and deliver in the current sprint.

2. The Plan for delivering the increment

The sprint backlog also contains a plan for delivering the increment and achieving the sprint goal.

In simple words, it is a plan for how the team expects to complete the work and achieve the sprint goal.

It highlights the work required to be done in order to meet the sprint goal.

It also provides guidance regarding the delivery of the items. This means the plan includes information on:

- What specific tasks are required to complete the work?

- What type of work is required?

- What work is assigned to each member?

High Priority Process Improvement

While the shortlisted items and the plan for delivering the increment are the most important sprint backlog items, there is also another useful component.

The sprint backlog also contains at least one high priority process improvement. The process improvements refer to suggestions on how to improve processes and how to perform better quality work.

Process improvements are identified during the sprint retrospective of the previous sprint and are then included in the sprint backlog of the next sprint to help improve the work performance.

Sprint Backlog and the Development Team

The sprint backlog belongs solely to the development team.

This statement means that the sprint backlog is managed ONLY by the development team. It is made by and for the developers exclusively.

Only the development team can make changes to the sprint backlog. They may also add more work to the sprint backlog. New work is usually added in order to achieve the sprint goal. As the team develops more clarity about the project, they may discover that more work is required to complete the product's features and achieve the sprint goal. Therefore, the team adds new work to the sprint backlog to increase their chances of achieving the objective of the sprint.

However, do note that the development team would not readily add any work that does not support the sprint goal.

Creating a new Sprint Goal for the New Sprint

For the new sprint, the scrum team would create a new sprint backlog. After completing a sprint, the team has an opportunity to reprioritize the project and decide which items require their attention the most. This is why a new sprint backlog consisting of a new sprint goal, shortlisted product backlog items, and a plan will be created for a new sprint.

INCREMENT

An increment can be described in many ways. An increment is:

- A deliverable that is created by the development team in a sprint.
- The outcome of what the team has been working on during the sprint.
- A stepping stone towards achieving the product goal.

When a product backlog item meets the definition of done, it becomes an increment. So basically, once a product backlog item has been worked on by the development team, its final version is referred to as an increment.

In more technical terms, an increment can be described as the sum of all product backlog items completed from the current sprint and value of the increments from previous sprints.

Let's look at it another way:

Increment = Finished product backlog items from current sprint + Finished product backlog items from previous sprints

In other words, you may consider that the sprint is the new work that is done in the current sprint, which is added to the already existing work from the previous sprint.

Example of an Increment: Car Manufacturing

Next, let's look at an easy and simplified example.

Let's say you're making a sports car, like a Ferrari. To make the car, we will first split the work into multiple sprints:

1. Sprint 1: Body
2. Sprint 2: Body + Wheels
3. Sprint 3: Body + Wheels + Engine

Now let's explore what exactly is happening during each of these sprints.

Sprint 1 Increment: Body

In the first sprint, you would make the body, and this would be your increment at the end of the first sprint. At this point there is no engine, no interior and no wheels.

Sprint 2 Increment: Body + Wheels

In the second sprint, you would add the wheels. Note that the body is the increment from the first sprint, and you created the wheels in this sprint. Therefore, the body AND the wheels would be the increment for the second sprint.

Sprint 3 Increment: Body + Wheels + Engine

In the third sprint, you would add the engine.

Do remember that the increment is the sum of all of what you have previously created + currently created.

The previous increment would include the body and the wheels, while you have just recently created the engine in the current sprint.

Therefore, the body, wheels plus the engine, would be the increment for the 3rd sprint.

Sprint 3 Increment = Previous increments + 3rd sprint increment (Body + Wheels) + (Engine)

Points to Remember

- Every increment must be done, this means that your deliverables must be complete and in usable condition, they cannot be half finished.

- An increment should meet the scrum team's definition of done. This means that it should satisfy the team's perspective about what constitutes a finished product according to their criteria.

- Furthermore, every increment must be releasable. By releasable, we mean the increment should be usable on its own, and it should be able to function on its own.

- The increment must be completed and fully functional, regardless of whether it is actually released or not.

DEFINITION OF DONE (DOD)

What is the Definition of Done (DOD)?

The definition of done refers to having a shared understanding for what it means for the work to be complete. The scrum guide states that on a project, everyone should understand what done means.

Think of the definition of done as a quality requirement that you need to fulfill. The DOD formally describes the state of the increment when it meets the criteria and quality standards required for the product. In simple words, the DOD is a checklist of criteria for product completion. It is the acceptance criteria for the product.

The DOD contains the list of requirements that must be met for the product to be considered as complete. Fulfilling the DOD means the product has satisfied all requirements for it to be accepted by the team as well as the customer. When a product backlog item meets the definition of done, it becomes an increment. If a product backlog item does not meet the definition of done, it is not released. Furthermore, it should not be presented at the sprint review either and should instead be returned to the product backlog.

By sharing the same thoughts and ideas about the criteria for product completion, scrum team members can develop better transparency about the work they're doing.

The DOD is also used as a tool for assessing whether the work on the increment has been completed.

For example, in the case of a software project e.g., an application, game, website etc, the DOD can be a checklist of features and activities. The product would only be considered complete after you've completed the entire checklist.

Definition of Done (DOD) Example

✓ Write Code

✓ Provide comments on code

✓ Perform QA

✓ Performance Testing

✓ Resolve Issues

✓ Update Documents

✓ Deploy Project

What happens when multiple Scrum teams are working on a product?

Always remember that scrum teams are expected to have a common understanding of the definition of done.

If there are multiple scrum teams working on a product, then they should mutually define the definition of done and comply with it. You need to ensure every team member has the same view on what "done" means.

If each member of every development team knows the exact requirements for product completion, this would increase the chances of creating the correct product and decrease the chances of failure.

However, if multiple teams are following a different definition of done, there is risk of creating products that might have errors and the wrong specifications.

Who creates the Definition of Done?

The entire scrum team creates the definition of done together.

The scrum guide states that if the definition of done is already a part of the guidelines of the organization doing the project, then the teams are expected to just follow that as a minimum.

On the other hand, if the organization does not have a definition of done in its guidelines, the scrum team is expected to create a definition of done by themselves.

When should you decide on a Definition of Done?

The discussion on the definition of done needs to happen at the beginning of the project. All the scrum team members come together to have a discussion to decide what it means for a chunk of work to be done.

Stringent Criteria for higher quality

Over time, as the team develops a better understanding of the project, they can have a stricter criterion for the definition of done.

Therefore, the definition of done can change and evolve to include stricter criteria for developing higher quality products.

The definition of done can change and evolve as time goes by and it doesn't need to stay fixed forever.

To summarize,

- The DOD helps us evaluate when the work has been completed.
- It helps us develop transparency by developing a shared understanding of completed work.

RELEASE PLANNING

Before understanding release planning, we must first understand the meaning of a release.

What is a release?

A release can either be a single increment or a series of increments. Furthermore, a release is usually a high priority product feature that is essential for the product. Basically, it is a very valuable feature of the product that you're developing.

What is release planning?

Once the development team creates some of the high priority items from the product backlog, you will end up with a working product that you can actually release into the market. Therefore, release planning refers to deciding what qualifies as a useable product that can be released into the market.

Release planning example: Smartphone

Let's say you're making a smartphone. How would you decide when is the right time to release it into the market?

Consider that in a single increment, you create a phone with a voice calling feature. You could release this phone into the market with only a single feature, or you could wait and add more features before releasing it. For example, you could add a high-powered camera in future increments. Therefore, you also have the choice of releasing it after a **series of increments**.

Customers love value addition and the more value your product offers in people's lives, the greater the chances of it being successful.

Who makes the decision for release planning?

The final decision for release planning lies with the product owner. The product owner decides whether to release a version with the basic features, or whether it is better add a couple of more features before launching the product into the market.

Is every increment release worthy?

Should we release a product every time we update it?

Should we release the product into the market after every sprint?

It is not necessary to release every increment after every sprint. It might be that you decide to have 4 increments before you decide on a release. For example, you must have noticed whenever smartphone companies like apple or Samsung release the newest software update, sometimes it contains a large number of new features and at other times, it can contain very few new features. So the decision to release an increment varies from situation to situation.

At the end of the day, it depends on the product owner's decision. The product owner may or may not decide to release the increment.

BURNDOWN CHART

A burndown chart represents the amount of work left to complete the project, versus time.

It helps you measure the progress of the team and evaluate how much work has been completed so far and how much work is left to be done.

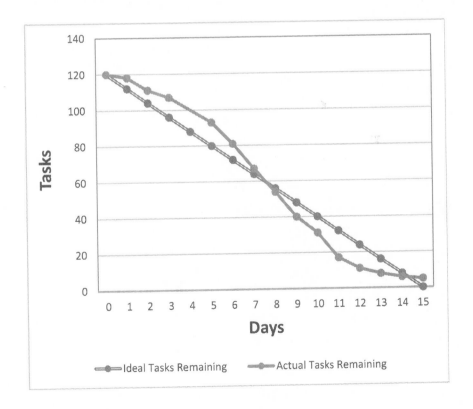

The X axis shows time, usually represented by the number of days.

The Y axis shows the work left to be done, which is represented by the number of tasks.

There is also a starting point, which shows the total number of tasks to be done on the project. In this case, we see the starting point at 120 tasks, towards the top left corner of the chart.

Notice the two lines on the chart, ideal tasks remaining, and actual tasks remaining.

Ideal tasks remaining show you the ideal case scenario of how many tasks we **should** have completed by this time.

Actual tasks remaining shows how many tasks we have actually been able to complete in reality.

As work gets done, the number of tasks will decrease, and the number of days will increase. For example, we started the project with 120 tasks on day 1 and by the 6th day, we have 80 actual tasks remaining. This means from day 1 to day 6, we have completed 40 tasks.

In short, as the burndown chart proceeds, the y axis (number of tasks) decreases while the x axis (no. of days) increases.

There are also 2 situations worth noting in a burndown chart:

- If the actual work/tasks line is above the ideal work/tasks line, it means there is more work left to be done, and that we are running behind schedule.
- For example, observe the chart on day 5, the actual tasks remaining are 93, while the ideal tasks remaining are 80. This means that we should have been able to complete 13 (93-80) more tasks by this time. Therefore, it means we are running

behind schedule and we need to get more work done as we are running behind our initial plan.

- If the actual tasks remaining line is below the ideal tasks remaining line, it means there is less work to be done, and we are ahead of schedule.

- For example, take a look at day 11. The ideal tasks remaining are 32, while the actual tasks remaining are 17. This means that by this point in time, we have gotten more work done on the project. We have lesser work that remains to be completed compared to what was originally expected and planned. We are ahead of schedule as we have completed 15 extra tasks (32-17).

USER STORIES

In scrum, project work is broken down into user stories.

A user story is a feature or functionality of the product. It describes the requirements and value of the product from the customer/stakeholder's perspective.

User stories describe the features of a software/technical product in simple everyday language. They are written from the perspective of the end user and explain how the feature will provide value to the customer.

User stories are much more useful compared to technical documentations of product specifications. This is because user stories are written in the form of a simple explanation of what we are trying to do on the project. This makes them understandable for everyone involved on the project. Through user stories, developers can easily understand what the customer wants and they can use this information to create products that best fulfill the customers requirements.

In comparison, if the customer describes the product in terms of technical details or specifications, there is a chance the developers and customers will not be able to understand each other. Therefore, user stories help bridge the gap between their understanding.

In other words, user stories make communication easier between technical and business sides of the project. Lets quickly summarize what we've learned.

Developers (Technical): User stories make it easy for the developers to understand what customers are looking for and what kind of a feature would fulfil their requirements.

Customers (Business): User stories make it easier for the customers to explain clearly of what exactly they want.

User Story Template

Next, let's learn how to make a user story template. First, it is important to know that user stories are written from the perspective of the user, this is the person who is actually going to be using the product.

Most user stories can be divided into 3 parts: 1. Role 2. Goal and 3. Benefit.

I'm going to share a simple format you can use to create user stories:

The sentence for a user story has 3 parts:

- As a
- I want to
- So that

As a ----- Role (As a - represents the role of the person)

I want to ----- Goal/Deliverable (I want to - represents the goal you want to achieve or the deliverable you want

So that ----- Benefit (So that – represents the benefit or advantage you want to get out of it)

User Story Examples

Let's take the example of a user story of a customer for an e-commerce website.

You would say:

- As a - customer
- I want to - add products to my cart
- So that - i can buy as many items as I want to

Next, let's say if you're making a social media app and you had to create a user story of a customer.

- As a - Social media user
- I want to - See people's hobbies
- So that - I can be friends with the people who like the same things as I do

By using user stories, it is easier to figure what kind of feature you need to develop which can solve your user's problem.

Difference between User Stories and Product Backlog items

A product backlog contains a list of everything that needs to be done on the project.

This includes user stories as well as things like bug fixes, enhancements, change requests, and other various things to be done on the project. Every item in the product backlog is known as a PBI, or product backlog item.

On the other hand, user stories specifically refer to the features and functionality required by the customer/end user.

STORY POINTS

To estimate the overall time and effort required to complete the project, the development team makes use of story points.

During the sprint, the development team estimates the work required on the project. To do this, the team evaluates the size of all the user stories to check how much effort and time commitment is required to complete each one of them.

The sum total of the story points of all the user stories represents the overall time and effort to complete the project.

What are Story Points?

Story points represent the effort required to complete the user story.

Each user story is assigned story points.

Also, note that story points measure the size and complexity of the user story.

Sizing a user story involves taking the following aspects into consideration:

- Amount of work: How much work is required to complete it?
- Complexity: How difficult and challenging is it?

- Time: How much time would it take?
- Risk: What is the amount of uncertainty involved?

How to estimate Story Points

To estimate the value of a story point, the development team defines one user story as a baseline.

Let's look at how we would go about it:

- First, list down all the user stories.
- Then, organize them from smallest to largest.
- Next, choose the baseline user story. For the baseline, you should choose a user story that everyone on the team is familiar with.
- You will now use the baseline story to estimate all the other stories.
- After that, you will pick the next user story and determine whether it is bigger or smaller than the baseline story.

Mostly, story points use different scales for sizing. The different scales include:

- Linear Scale - 1,2,4,8,16
- X-Small, Small, Medium, Large, Extra-Large
- Fibonacci scale - 0, 0.5, 1, 2, 3, 5, 8, 13, 20, 40,100.

Example: Dinner Party

1. **List user stories**
   a. Pasta
   b. Pizza

   c. Burgers

2. Choose baseline

- Pasta – 2 Story points

3. Choose next user story

- Pizza - 4 Story points

Explanation

Let's look at an easy example.

Consider you're having an amazing and tasty dinner party and you're making delicious Italian food for your guests.

First, you would start off by listing all the dishes or user stories you're going to make. Assume we will be making 3 different dishes today:

1. Pasta
2. Pizza
3. Burgers

You've got a list of different foods, but you would choose only one of them as a baseline.

To select the baseline, it is recommended to use a simple and easy to understand task that all team members can relate to and are potentially skilled at.

For example, if everyone on the team knows how to make pasta, you should choose it as a baseline.

Let's assume the team estimates that the pasta is worth 2 story points.

- Pasta = 2 Story points

- Choose pasta as the baseline

You will now use pasta as a baseline to estimate all the other items.

Our next user story is a pizza.

The team can now compare both user stories and evaluate which one requires more effort, the pasta or the pizza.

If the pizza requires more effort and is more complex to make, the team will assign more story points to it than the baseline user story.

Because the team has already agreed on a baseline and understands how much work is required for it, they can easily estimate how much effort is required for the next task based on their knowledge of the baseline task.

In this example, the team assigns 4 story points to the pizza. This means that according to the team, making the pizza is worth twice the effort of making pasta.

Pizza = 4 Story points (Twice the effort required to make pasta)

This is how you will estimate the story points for all the user stories in your product backlog. Remember that you can just as easily use this method on a software project. Just replace the pizza and the pasta with any of the tasks involved on your software project, for example coding, designing, or quality assurance.

In the same way, if you're working on an application or a software product, you should first choose a baseline task. Then, think about how all the other tasks compare to it and give them story points accordingly.

Why story points don't consider time?

Story points don't consider work in terms of days, hours or minutes. Instead of estimating in hours, the team looks at the effort required to complete the work.

The reason is that different project teams have different experience and productivity levels.

Let's say there are 2 development teams from separate companies, and they are both given a programming task.

One team might be able to complete the programming in 5 hours while the other might do the same task in 8 hours.

To create a more realistic estimate, it is better to consider the effort required rather than the time involved to do the work.

Project Uncertainty

Iterative Projects	Predictive Projects
Software development	**Construction (Bridges)**
• Uncertainty	• More Clarity
• Expected to change	• Easier to estimate in specific man hours
• Work is difficult to estimate precisely	• Time taken per task

Another reason why story points don't consider time is because of the uncertainty that comes with every project.

Agile and iterative projects like software development have more uncertainty and are always expected to change. That is why work is difficult to estimate precisely in such projects.

Because of this, it is not convenient for the development team to mention specific time frames for work that does not have a lot of clarity.

On the other hand, predictive projects, e.g. projects that involve the construction of buildings and bridges, have more clarity in terms of their tasks. Having clarity about the scope of the work makes it easier to estimate how much time it would take to complete the task in specific man hours.

Therefore, for agile projects, story points are more useful. They are a relative measure based on the team's own credentials.

The team decides their estimates based on their own experience, productivity levels and the amount of effort they would need to put in to complete the tasks.

Absolute Hours

Absolute hours are another method for estimation.

If you have more clarity on the work you're doing, you can use absolute hours for estimation. This method is most useful for estimating the specific and known tasks that your team is very familiar with.

Absolute hours allocate specific time frames for tasks. For example, for designing a software application you can allocate hours as follows:

Designing – 8 hours

Programming – 16 hours

Example

Consider a situation where your team starts working on a new project and they realize they have previously worked on a project with similar specifications before.

Because of your team's prior experience of working on a similar project, they would have more clarity about the time it takes to complete each task on the new project as well. This will help the team allocate absolute hours to the tasks they are familiar with.

Conclusion

To conclude, at the end of the day, it is up to the development team to decide the estimation method and whether they size the project in terms of story points or absolute hours.

You should use what suits you best depending on how clear the tasks on the project are.

VELOCITY

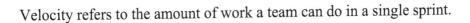

Velocity refers to the amount of work a team can do in a single sprint.

It is calculated at the end of a sprint and is the sum of all completed user stories in a sprint.

Velocity determines how much work a team can comfortably take on and complete for a single sprint.

The major benefit of velocity is that it allows the team to estimate how long the project will take to complete, based on how much work the team can do in a single sprint.

It is not recommended for a team to take on more work than their velocity. Taking on more work than a team's velocity would exceed the capacity of the team and they would not be able to finish and deliver the work.

How to Calculate Velocity

Let's look at an example of how we can calculate velocity for a project.

Consider that you're working on a software project codenamed X and you have a sprint coming up. Your team starts off by picking user stories to work on for the sprint.

If you may remember, user stories are the product features you are developing for your customers.

The diagram shows the list of user stories of Project X. It shows how many story points each user story is worth, e.g. Feature A is worth 2 story points.

User Stories of Project X

Feature A – 2 Story points   **(Completed)**

Feature B – 2 Story points   **(Completed)**

Feature C – 4 Story points   **(Completed)**

Feature D – 5 story points   **(Incomplete)**

The team picks Feature A, B, C and D to work on in this sprint.

Let's say that, you were able to complete Features A, B and C. However, you were not able to complete Feature D.

What would be your team's velocity for this sprint?

Your velocity would be the sum of all the story points of the work you were able to complete in one sprint.

It is important to note that incomplete user stories are not added to velocity and its calculation.

Velocity = Sum of all story points in one sprint

Velocity = Feature A story points + Feature B story points + Feature C story points

    = 2+2+4

    = 8

This means the team has a velocity of 8 story points.

Your team can comfortably develop features or user stories worth 8 points in each sprint.

What would happen if the team decides to work on more than 8 points in a sprint, for example 15 points?

This would be difficult for your team because it exceeds their capacity. Your team can only afford to manage work which is worth 8 story points in total.

On the other hand, what happens if your team picks less than 8 story points for a sprint? For example, what if they pick 3 story points for the current sprint?

This means you can still take on 5 more story points because you have spare capacity available and can easily get more work done.

Estimating the No. of Sprints required for project completion

Next, we will learn about how you can use velocity to estimate the number of sprints needed to complete the project.

Assume there you're working on developing a software and you have a product backlog in which you have user stories worth 24 story points.

Product backlog for new software:

- Feature A – 4 story points
- Feature B – 4 story points
- Feature C – 8 story points
- Feature D – 8 story points

Total story points – 4+4+8+8 = 24

If your team has a velocity of 8, how many sprints would you require to complete the project?

Sprints = Total user story points / Velocity

In other words,

No. of sprints required to complete project = Total user story points / Velocity per sprint

= 24 / 8

= 3 Sprints

THANK YOU

Congratulations on completing the book. It is my hope that you have upgraded yourself with knowledge on agile and scrum and will be able to approach projects more confidently.

Best of luck for your PSM exam, I would love to see you become certified soon.

I wish you the best in everything you do and everywhere you go.

Umer W.

Made in the USA
Middletown, DE
08 December 2023

44950720R00090